materially
crafted

A DIY PRIMER FOR
THE DESIGN-OBSESSED

VICTORIA HUDGINS

PHOTOGRAPHY BY JOCELYN NOEL

STC CRAFT | A MELANIE FALICK BOOK | NEW YORK

Published in 2015 by Stewart, Tabori & Chang
An imprint of ABRAMS.

Library of Congress Control Number: 2014942955
ISBN: 978-1-61769-140-9

Photographs by Jocelyn Noel unless otherwise noted.
Photographs on page 43 by I Spy Photography, page 60 by Athena Plichta,
page 82 by Tina Fussell, page 113 by Lemaire Photography, and page 140 by Pictilio.
Cover photograph by Chelsea McNamara.
Illustrations by Amanda Waggoner.

Editor: Cristina Garces
Designer: Sarah Gifford
Production Manager: Denise LaCongo

The text of this book was composed in Bodoni, Dolly, and Neutra.

Printed and bound in China
10 9 8 7 6 5 4 3 2 1

ABRAMS
THE ART OF BOOKS SINCE 1949

115 West 18th Street
New York, NY 10011
www.abramsbooks.com

WITHDRAWN

This book is dedicated to my daughter,
who wants to learn how to do
everything all at once. May we all,
like her, jump into crafting hands first.

contents

I

SECTION ONE

the basics

SECTION TWO

materials + projects

introduction

HOW MANY TIMES HAVE YOU STARTED a craft project and never quite gotten around to finishing it? How many times have you laughed at the blogs featuring Pinterest "fails" only to be grateful that your own fails never made it online? Over the years, I've talked with many readers of my blog, *A Subtle Revelry*, and learned that many of them have very long lists of projects, crafts, and tasks they want to tackle, but no clear plan for how to see these things through. In fact, they have little hope that many of their ideas will actually become a reality. Why is this?

It is certainly not from lack of inspiration, nor lack of materials. Lack of time perhaps, but then again we all seem to make time for the things we really want to see through. No, over the past two years of interacting with readers, blogging, and pinning, I have come to learn that the reason we stall out on great ideas is because we lack a foundation of skills—we need a guide to lead us. Guides teach us how to accomplish what we desire and encourage us to develop the right techniques.

It always begins the same: We see a pretty photo, we click the link. We read a post that starts with "melt the wax" and we freeze because we don't really know how to melt wax, what kind of wax to use (*is it different from the wax we—painfully—experience at the salon?* we wonder), or where to buy the wax.

We then search "working with wax" online and come upon article after article of technical jargon that often contradicts itself, and is full of unrelated keywords and obnoxious ads. We get discouraged, downhearted, and quickly put aside the original idea we had to be creative, to make something new and unique with our hands. And we return to scrolling through the pin boards, seeing great ideas and dreaming about accomplishing them someday.

So here's the question: What if you had a guide to lead you through these photos and posts? A guide that could take you back to basics and teach, in simple language, the skills needed to work with a foundation of simple materials to produce projects mirroring the beautiful inspiration you find online? A guide to take you through the process and give you the ability to stumble upon any photo and make it a reality in your own life?

Rustic Wood Bunting, page 116

That is what I hope this book becomes for you. A guide to take along with you on your blog-hopping, Pinterest-scrolling, Instagram-idea-making adventures. Each chapter is devoted to a different common craft material, so that you are ready to tackle any project that you find online or in the bookstore. I have also included a lookbook at the end of each chapter which showcases other gorgeous DIY projects that have inspired me from some of my favorite bloggers and pinners. From finding inspiration to getting prepared and gathering the right tools, *Materially Crafted* will teach you to create the amazing projects you've always wanted for your own materially crafted home!

ON FINDING inspiration

If you are looking for a treasure trove of crafting inspiration, I hope this book will help by encouraging you to play around with materials you may not have thought to use before. I find that often it's the actual work of starting a project that ends up inspiring me in many new and different ways. So if you are feeling stuck for inspiration, my greatest piece of advice would be to get crafting: Just. Start. Something. Now! Here are a few other tips I have for staying creative and getting inspired:

❶ DO SOMETHING DIFFERENT

I always seem to find new inspiration when I break up my current routine. Read a new genre, go to a new type of event, eat at a new restaurant, pick a new material from this book to explore, or go to a new park with the kids. Enliven your senses to new experiences, and you will pick up inspiration as you go. In my opinion, routine is the enemy of creativity.

❷ WALK (OR BIKE) A NEW NEIGHBORHOOD

This tip could easily be translated as: Travel. Experiencing new cultures is the singlemost inspiring thing a creative person can do. However, with kids, work, and everyday life, it is not always possible to jet-set around the world. In the meantime, exploring new neighborhoods in your own town can be quite inspiring.

❸ READ INTERNATIONAL MAGAZINES

I try to make time every so often to catch up on a couple of my favorite international magazines, like *Vogue Living Australia* and *Elle Décor*. I find the scope of ideas in these magazines is greater since many American magazines take their stories from the same sites I read daily. When reading them, go beyond the explicit and write down the names of inspiring photographers, stylists, and products to research later. Many of my conceptual ideas, pins, and projects come from exploring this world of media.

Large Concrete Planters, page 54

④ EXPOSE YOURSELF TO ART

Museums are great resources but concerts and dance performances can be just as inspiring. Anywhere you can find art around you, soak it up and jot down what you love for later.

⑤ SHOP VINTAGE

One of my favorite inspiring activities is to shop vintage stores. Walking around, dreaming about repurposing items, and seeing the designs of the past have a way of really jogging my creative side. And never skip the book section! Home design pre-1980 is so fun to read about and always inspires a new project or two for me.

⑥ DRINK COFFEE AND LAY IN BED UNTIL 3 A.M.

This one happens more often by mistake, when I forget that having caffeine after 2 P.M. is a great recipe for insomnia. My most creative ideas come when my body is at rest and my mind is racing. Next time you are up past midnight, try brainstorming about an upcoming project and write down what you dream up. Just be sure to erase 40 percent of the crazed, middle-of-the-night thoughts the next morning.

⑦ GO FOR A DRIVE

Driving has a very cathartic effect on my mind. It redirects the left side of my brain and allows the right, creative side, to let loose. Distracting your brain from the problem at hand can often spark a burst of creative genius, so go out and take a drive if you're feeling uninspired.

⑧ FIND SOMETHING AT HOME TO MAKE AWESOME

Take something you currently have in your home that you don't love and challenge yourself to remake it into something you do! Once every few months, I go through the house and pick out pieces that are "almost" awesome. I set them on a table in the garage and begin to envision what would make them spectacular. Often, a new coat of paint, a change of fabric, or switching up how I use the item is all I need to make many pieces in my home much more useful to me. I love having plants around the house, but was recently underwhelmed by the pots I had. Forcing myself to envision the plants in different planters made me realize the rustic look of concrete would help them look awesome next to just about anything, and inspired the Large Concrete Planters on page 54.

Colorful Rolled Tea Lights, page 102

ON CHOOSING a project

Taking inspiration and turning it into reality is the hardest part about embarking on a new DIY project. When you begin to plan craft projects there are many factors to take into consideration, the most important of which are the amount of time you have to put something together, your budget for materials, and your current skill set. Have you ever finished a project and sat there wondering why it looks so different than the photo online? It's important to achieve a balance between expectation and reality, and projects often fail because one or more of these factors are off.

After you've assessed these factors, determining your vision is the next crucial step. One of the best and worst products of the incredible wealth of inspiration online is that too much inspiration can quickly translate into too much clutter! Before you embark on starting any craft, stop and ask yourself the larger questions: How will this particular idea fit into my life? How will it be beneficial to me? How will it make me feel when it's complete? Not everything in life has to be functional in the traditional sense, but everything you bring into your home should function to make your life more beautiful.

The best reason to become a more proficient crafter is that once you have a solid foundation, there's no end to your options for customizing any project to suit your needs! As you are looking for projects and inspiration, don't bypass something because the color isn't what you'd choose or the design doesn't quite suit your whimsy. Note the ideas and concepts and learn to design and re-create them in a way that adds beauty, value, and function to your home.

ON HAVING the right tools

After you've determined your vision, and before you begin crafting and creating, it is important to make sure your toolbox is properly stocked. There is nothing worse than being halfway through a project only to realize you don't have a tool necessary for completing it (you wouldn't try to make a new dish in the kitchen without making sure you had all the ingredients, would you?). When starting a new craft project, first read through all of the instructions once, then clear off a workspace and lay out all of your materials and tools in a cute and inspirational way—you won't believe how much this will help you in seeing your project through.

A downfall to many online tutorials is that materials lists often focus only on materials used for the actual project, but leave out tools that are needed to *construct* the project. While you won't always have every item in your stash already, here are the craft tools I use the most. Use this list to make sure your box is stocked before embarking on the projects in this—or any—book or online.

SCISSORS

The vast majority of crafts will require scissors at some point. They are important—their strength and sharpness or lack thereof can easily take your ideal project and turn it into a success or a failure. I like to keep four different pairs on hand for a variety of uses:

FABRIC SCISSORS: If you will be doing any fabric work or sewing, a good pair of fabric scissors is incredibly important. Choose 8" (20-cm) scissors with a strong metal blade and *only* use them on your fabric. Fabric scissors will quickly dull when used on other materials, and they need to be sharp to give you crisp, even lines. Store them in a cotton bag or sheath when not in use. (Note: Hide them from the family so they are not used for opening packages of chicken in a pinch—lesson learned from experience.) To sharpen dull scissors you can purchase a sharpening kit from your local craft store, or for an easy DIY solution, fold a piece of aluminum foil over about 4 times and cut through the piece with your scissors 4 to 5 times. It's a cheap fix that works really well! I tend to sharpen my scissors every 3 months or so, depending on how often I find myself cutting fabric.

DETAIL SCISSORS: For thread cutting, intricate paper crafting, and other detail-oriented projects, a set of small scissors provides nice, quick cuts. For these projects, my favorite scissors are 4" (10-cm) floral scissors, which you can pick up at any local garden store. They have a very sharp tip and are great for cuts when the detail of the snip is important.

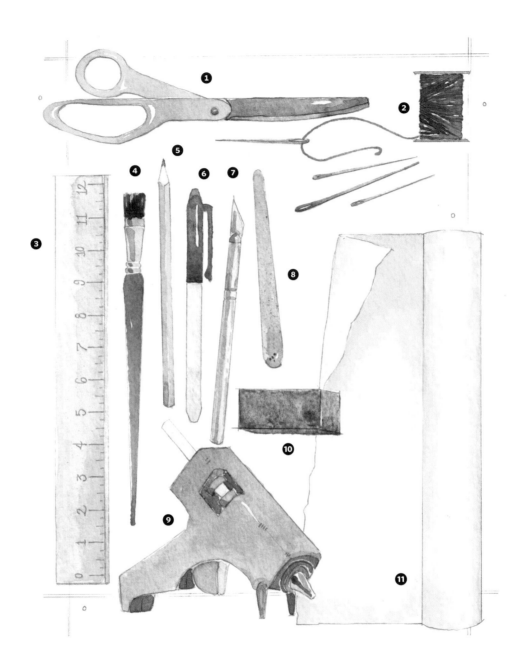

1 SCISSORS

2 NEEDLE AND THREAD

3 RULER

4 PAINTBRUSH

5 PENCIL

6 SHARPIE

7 X-ACTO KNIFE

8 NAIL FILE

9 HOT GLUE GUN

10 ERASER

11 WAXED PAPER

CRAFT SCISSORS: Everyday crafting scissors are another necessary addition to the tool-box. These should be sharpened quarterly (or every 25 projects) for prime usage. Craft scissors can be sharpened the same way that sewing scissors are sharpened, although I find sandpaper often works better than aluminum for these thinner blades. Use medium-grade sandpaper and try cutting through a sheet of waxed paper afterwards to lubricate the blade. Find a pair that measure 6 to 8" (15 to 20 cm) and have a firm, comfortable handhold. These can be used on paper and other crafting materials.

WIRE CUTTERS: These are great for cutting floral wire and other thick wire, as well as firmer materials like cardboard.

THREAD

Thread is a material that is usually purchased as needed for craft projects; however, I always keep a long length of white kitchen twine, a roll of fishing wire, and one skein of bright pink embroidery floss on hand. Thread is one of the materials most often left out of craft project instructions, so having a couple of basic colors and types on hand will help combat any unexpected omissions.

NEEDLES

I keep a package of embroidery needles on hand for last-minute fixes. Embroidery needles (also called crewel needles) are similar to hand-sewing needles except the eye of the needle is larger and the tip is slightly more blunt. The wide eye makes it easier to thread the needle for quick detail additions or necessary adjustments.

WAXED PAPER

While not normally considered a craft necessity, I use waxed paper just as much as anything else in my toolbox. A length of waxed paper torn from a roll you picked up at the grocery store will protect your work surface, preventing spilled paint from staining or drips of wax from sticking to your table. Waxed paper will also keep colored clay from transferring its color to your work area. It's a go-to for all craft projects in my house, and a roll of it will keep you cleanly crafting away all day long.

HOT GLUE GUN

Although there are many types of glue, hot glue is by far my favorite. I know I am probably insane, but I think it might be the cure for all my crafting woes. It works to glue just about anything together—I've used it to hang photos, fix tears, and secure anything I need to at a moment's notice. (Needless to say, you'll also need hot glue sticks to keep the gun gluin'.) I would never start a craft project without my trusty glue gun nearby, loaded and ready to fire. See page 134 for more glue options.

ERASER

A basic pencil eraser is another tool that has many nontraditional uses beyond simply erasing an errant line. It is often a go-to for marking my spot to cut or glue on paper and fabric. An eraser makes a perfect last-minute pincushion to store needles and pins during craft time. A couple of cuts with an X-Acto knife turns an eraser into a custom stamp. Erasers clean up scuffs and dust quickly and can even restore the original shiny patina of aged metal pipes.

NAIL FILE

An accidental addition to my craft toolbox, my nail file happened to jump in one day and it was used so many times, I never took it out. A nail file is a nice substitute for a bone folder to be used for folding, bending, and creasing paper. It is helpful in situations where a small straight edge is needed and works wonderfully for popping out plaster, papier-mâché, or wax from molds. And it's also nice to have on hand since nice nails are often a casualty of the crafty lifestyle. I use a regular cardboard emery board, but a metal file would work as well.

X-ACTO KNIFE

An X-Acto knife works great on clay, hardened wax, paper, fabric, and thin wood for projects where detail is important. Choose a stable knife with a turning head that can be locked in place for the best results.

SHARPIE

A Sharpie is like a pencil on steroids for the crafter. I use my Sharpies for everything from making labels to "printing" on fabric (I have even used them to decorate phone covers and plates), to create trendy and personalized projects.

PENCIL

A pencil is an obvious choice for a crafting toolbox, but one I have often been left scrambling to find. Be sure to have a couple sharpened and close by before embarking on a new project.

RULER

A basic straight edge is an important addition to any craft toolbox. Use it to measure, draw, and crease as you go.

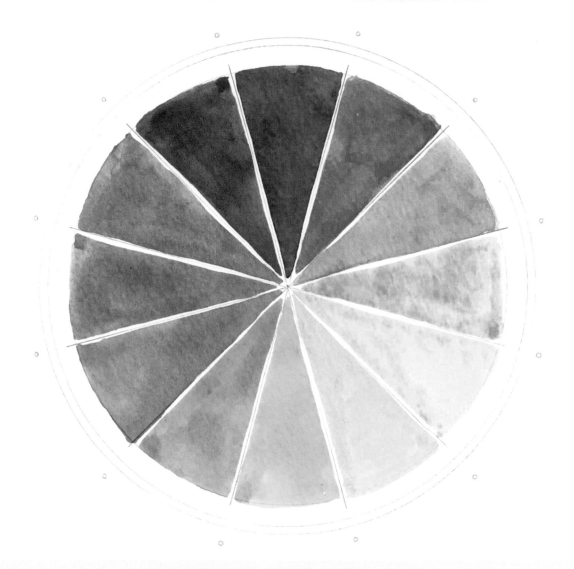

HOW TO PICK THE RIGHT COLOR

Knowing how to use the color wheel is invaluable for planning out your DIY projects. I often turn to mine when I'm trying to pick the perfect paint or paper colors to compliment a new craft. Although the color wheel contains multitudes of different hues, the slices of color shown here represent a smaller, more modern selection. When you're ready to choose hues for your own projects, use this wheel as a reference and follow my two rules of thumb:

❶ OPPOSITES ATTRACT

You can never go wrong by matching a color in your home with its opposite color on the wheel. Looking for a complementary color for your plum DIY dream? Look at the color directly across the wheel and you'll find that you're perfectly in style with a funky shade of green.

❷ COMPLEMENTS ARE WELCOME

If going opposite is not your style, choose a triad of colors that are all connected. Look at the colors directly to the right or directly to the left of the color of your choosing to create a classic combination that will always look great.

PAINTBRUSHES

Choosing the best paintbrush for the project is almost as important as the paint itself. A too thin, too thick, or too brittle brush can instantly take a piece from gallery worthy to preschool art project. You can use either natural- or synthetic-bristle brushes; the price and quality will vary by shape and material. Here are my favorite brush shapes:

ROUND: The round brush, or art brush, is what most people are accustomed to using. It has a nice round tip to allow paint to flow out of it smoothly and is great for painting on wood and canvas or other small projects.

FLAT: A flat brush produces pretty wide brushstrokes and is great for detail painting and creating stripes. It doesn't hold as much paint in the bristles as a round brush, so it works best on non-porous materials.

RIGGER: A rigger brush is very long and thin, making it perfect for handlettering or anything requiring a thin line.

ANGLE: An angle brush is used for creating sharp, bold lines and is the perfect brush to begin to experiment with texture painting. The brush is also great for painting sharp corners effortlessly, especially when creating arrows and geometric shapes.

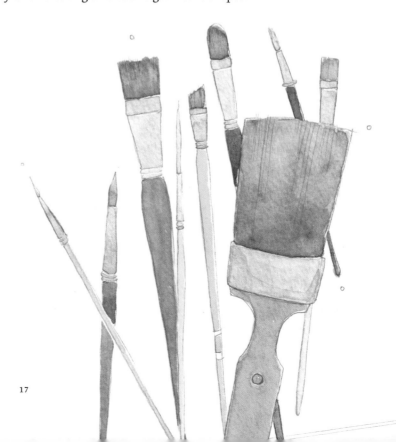

FROM LEFT TO RIGHT, BY TIP:
rigger, mop, flat, sword, angle,
filbert, painting, round, bright

FILBERT: A filbert brush has a rounded oval top. It can create thick or thin lines depending on how the brush is held and is best used for blending paints together. It is also my first choice when I need to paint glue onto a project because it disperses the glue well without clumping.

BRIGHT: A bright brush is a square-ish brush with short, firm hair that is easy to guide. It works great for creating shapes, getting into the nitty-gritty detail of a piece, or painting more advanced designs. This is also a good brush to use on metal since it will not slip or slide easily.

MOP: A mop brush is exactly what it sounds like—one with a whole mop of brush hair. It is wide and holds a lot of paint, making it a great option for watercolors and projects with a lot of freeform lines.

SWORD: A sword brush is a combination of the rigger and angle brushes. It is most often used for calligraphy. This brush creates a gorgeous striped effect when run down the length of wood, paper, or even fabric with the right type of paint.

PAINTING: A painting brush is a larger brush used most often for painting larger pieces. I find the large bristles of this brush best for use on flat surfaces, as they tend to fan out a bit when pressure is applied. It is a good brush to use for projects with taped-off designs because it creates clean lines and disperses paint evenly.

ON EXECUTING your ideas

Having the right tools is the first important step on the road to executing your vision. Here are a few other tips for ensuring your crafting experience is a success.

❶ PREP FOR THE MESS

Crafting is often a messy process, so always prep your area before beginning any project. Use an old bedsheet or tablecloth as a stand-in tarp that can easily be tossed afterward for the easiest clean-up, and keep a lint roller on hand for picking up small items, glitter, and dust. For small projects, a baking sheet lined with waxed paper will keep things stable and clean.

❷ MAKE IT WORK

Go into each new craft project with the mindset that you will just make it work, no matter what. Nothing can hinder a creative spirit more than a half-finished

French Knot Artwork, page 84

project. If you hit a road bump in the process, reevaluate and move forward. Even if the end result is different than you envisioned, a completed project will encourage more crafting.

③ CRAFT TO YOUR STYLE

No matter how great an idea, if it doesn't fit your style, you will not love it. Don't ever start a project just because it was popular online or someone awesome did it. Craft projects that truly fit your life and style are the ones you'll find yourself using time and time again, and will encourage you to continue creating more unique items in the future.

④ GIVE IT TIME

Crafting can be an amazing way to bring personality into your home and life. Instead of purchasing a premade version, creating it yourself (potentially from found objects) is a fabulous way to reduce, reuse, and challenge yourself to explore your creativity. *But*—can I tell you a secret? Crafting is not always cheap and hardly ever speedy. When beginning a project, be sure to budget the time and money that will actually be needed to get it accomplished, or you will be left feeling frustrated instead of excited about the final result.

spray paint

SPRAY PAINT IS ONE OF THE MOST COMMON and easiest materials to use to quickly transform an everyday object into a well-designed and gorgeous addition to your home. It is also a material that is often misused, and the line between gorgeous gloss and a hideous hue is a very thin one. When applied correctly, spray paint can make an impact on any space like nothing else. Although there are many methods for applying paint out there, I've found spray painting to be the most approachable method for a new crafter. When it comes to your time and money, there is no better option than picking a type of paint you love and spraying it on. And with my tips for creating your own custom spray paint from any water-based paint, you'll be transforming your humdrum objects into colorful masterpieces in no time!

10 TIPS FOR PERFECT spray painting

❶ CLEAN AND PRIME YOUR SURFACE

Spray paint will adhere to any surface it can, so if your project has a smidge of dirt or a spot of lint on it, it will become a permanent part of your piece. Before you pull out the paint, first clean and dry your piece and remove all leftover residue with a simple lint brush for a smooth and finished look. Then, add a coat of primer. This will give your project a better finish, and it helps hide any defects on the original surface.

❷ TAKE NOTE OF THE WEATHER

Spray paint applied when it is higher than 85°F (29°C) outside (especially in direct sunlight) will crack and break. Spray paint applied anywhere near freezing will glop dry. For best results, paint when the temperature is 60 to 80°F (16 to 27°C). When the weather is not cooperating, painting should be done in a garage or other covered, ventilated area.

❸ MAKE AN INFINITY SIGN

Many spray paint directions will recommend using a back and forth motion, but I have found making a wide infinity sign (which looks like a sideways 8) to be the best approach. It creates a clean finish and prevents the horrible end line that often occurs when spray painting in a back and forth, horizontal motion.

❹ BEAT IT UP A BIT

This technique is not for all projects. However, if you are going for an aged look, try beating your piece up a bit before you paint it. Use chains, nails, and other household items to mimic age marks on surfaces. Done well, this can result in adding a lovely vintage depth to your project. For a weathered look, leave the piece outdoors for a few weeks and "weather" it naturally before painting.

❺ BLOCK OVERSPRAY

You will probably remember to cover the pieces of your project that you don't want painted with painter's tape. However, spray paint travels farther than you think! Use full sheets of paper (or newspaper for large projects) to cover all the areas you do not want painted. Line the area you are painting with paper and tape it down to keep the rest of your project clean and paint-free.

6 STAY AWAY

Paint manufacturers suggest you spray 6 to 8" (15 to 20 cm) away from the project, so remember to keep your distance. Standing closer will leave your project gloopy and drip-ridden. For smaller projects, drop the piece into a deep cardboard box to remind you of the distance. For larger projects, I like to stand about 1' (30 cm) back from the object as I paint. This assures that I keep a good distance and provides consistent coverage throughout my painting.

7 KEEP A CLEAN NOZZLE

I currently have a collection of 57 spray paint cans, lined up and organized, awaiting their next project. I often use just a quarter or a half can for a project, so I keep my paint ready for next time by thoroughly cleaning out the sprayer nozzle after each use. It pops off easily and can be run through with water for a residue-free clean. If you do happen upon a can that has been clogged, use a cotton ball saturated with nail polish remover to clean out the nozzle—it works like magic.

8 DIP IT

Before you paint, dip your can of spray paint in hot water, submerging the entire lower half, for 5 minutes. The warmth of the water will thin out the paint, giving you a more even coating during the painting process.

9 HANDS OFF

Although the can says the paint might be dry to the touch in just a couple of hours, it will continue to cure for the next 1 to 5 days. The strong paint smell comes from the "off gassing" of the paint. As spray paint cures, the paint will deepen in color and set into the surface, and the smell will lessen. If possible, leave the painted project to dry until this smell disappears, signaling that your paint is fully cured.

10 SANDPAPER IS YOUR FRIEND

If you've followed all these tips, but your paint still ends up drippy or bubbles on you, fix it easily with a small amount of high-grit sandpaper (I like to use 220 count, meaning there are 220 abrasive particles per inch on the paper's surface). Gently sand down the affected area and repaint—no need to prime the area again. This also works if your paint ever gets chipped down the road. Write the brand and color used in pencil in a hidden spot on your project (in a drawer, under the chair), so that if and when the need for repainting arises, the matching paint will be easy to identify.

HOW TO MAKE YOUR OWN SPRAY PAINT

Many times, I stood in the spray paint aisle of my local hardware store wishing for a color that was not there, hoping a hue between hot pink and pale pink would pop out at me—a color as design-friendly as the project I had in mind. Then, in that same aisle, I discovered a simple tool. It allows you to combine whatever colors you want to make your own custom spray paint. Genius! The secret: a compression sprayer (because how else will you get the typography letters on her wall to match the exact ballet-pink she has been dreaming of?).

SUPPLIES

Compression sprayer
   (I use the Preval brand)
Small funnel
½ cup (4 oz / 118 ml) water-based
   paint in any hue
½ cup (4 oz / 118 ml) paint thinner

INSTRUCTIONS

1. Using the funnel, fill the sprayer base with the paint and paint thinner. Replace the closing cap and shake vigorously.

2. Remove the cap and install the compression sprayer nozzle on your sprayer base. Spray the paint following the 10 Tips for Perfect Spray Painting on page 22.

HOW TO mix colors

Any color you want to make can be achieved by mixing primary hues. Whether you are considering spray paint, acrylic, or watercolor, the color-mixing combinations always remain the same. Looking for a way to pale out that bright, heavy hue you've found? The chart below shows how adding small increments of a color (in our case, hot pink) will drastically change your beginning hue.

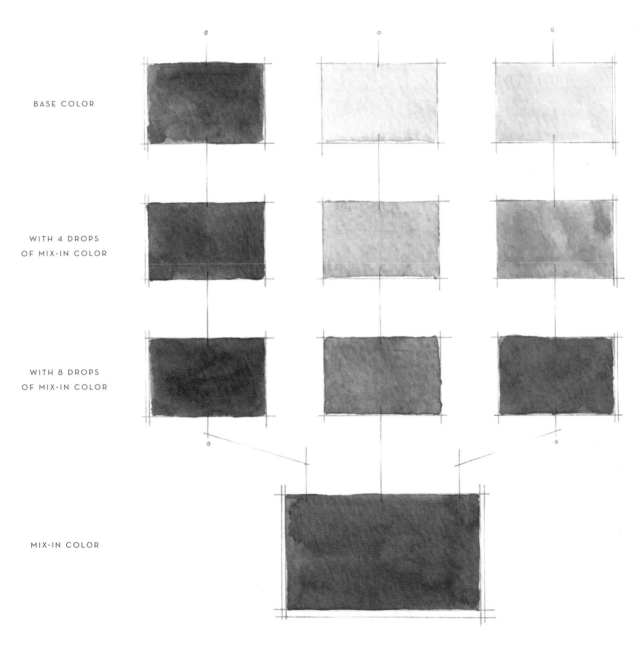

BASE COLOR

WITH 4 DROPS
OF MIX-IN COLOR

WITH 8 DROPS
OF MIX-IN COLOR

MIX-IN COLOR

HOW TO MAKE MILK PAINT

Milk paint is an organic form of paint that is especially useful when projects might come in contact with food. Since milk is the binder for the material, the paint is nontoxic and gives off no noxious vapors (or VOCs—volatile organic compounds). Milk paint is traditionally used to give an antique or distressed look to wood and terra-cotta; however, it can be mixed with bright pigments or food coloring to achieve a more vibrant effect on projects such as the Floral Drink Corks on page 28.

SUPPLIES

1 quart (960 ml) skim milk
Wide-mouth jar
Juice of 1 medium lemon
Slotted spoon
1 tablespoon all-purpose flour
Food coloring in color of your choice

INSTRUCTIONS

1. Place the milk in a large, wide-mouth jar or other container.

2. Pour the lemon juice into the milk, and let sit overnight.

3. The next day, skim the top with a large slotted spoon to remove any chunks of curdled milk.

4. Stir in the flour and about 10 drops of food coloring and mix. Add more food coloring as needed to achieve your desired pigment. Use within 12 hours to prevent spoiling.

NOTE: *The paint will smell sour when wet, but the odor disappears when dry.*

EIGHT THINGS YOU DIDN'T THINK YOU COULD SPRAY PAINT

I bet if you walked around your house right now, you'd find a bunch of places that could be completely changed with just a few sprays of paint! Here are eight ideas to get you started:

1 DOORKNOBS

Want a doorknob update without paying an arm and a leg for the new piece? Take the knobs off your doors and take them outside to be painted (weather permitting!). Three light coats in a gray, matte black, or glossy white paint will have your house feeling fresh again.

2 DRIED OR ARTIFICIAL PLANTS

Decorating with dried or artificial plants can be great since you don't need to care for them, but it's hard to get past the dead or overly faux look. Instead of fighting it, go with the vibe and add a few bright coats of paint, like we did with the Floral Drink Corks on page 28, to turn them into small works of art that you'll be proud to show off.

3 CURTAINS

Update your old curtains with a pop of paint. Use painter's tape to tape off two to four lines along the bottom of the curtains, then use fabric paint to create coordinating stripes.

4 CHANDELIERS

A few years back I bought a huge chandelier for $10 at a garage sale. We spray painted it for a photo shoot, and then painted it again, and then painted it again to be hung up at home. It is still one of my favorite pieces, and I love knowing it can take on a whole new color—and look—in just an afternoon. Just be sure to remove the lightbulbs and tape off the sockets and electrical points before spray painting.

5 UPHOLSTERED FURNITURE

Using a ratio of 1 part paint to 1 part fabric medium, you can actually paint directly on upholstered fabric, like the Spray-Painted Chair with Fabric Cushion on page 32, for a quick furniture update at home.

6 CANDLES

Painting candles is such a great way to brighten up the home, and perfect for making your everyday collection come alive for your next gathering of guests. Tape off the top third of the candle (including the wick) and paint the bottom two-thirds with our homemade sprayable milk paint (opposite) or an acrylic paint mix. Or, tape off as you go, and paint stripes, polka dots, or monograms onto candles of all sorts.

7 WALLS

Painting the walls is something we normally think of as only possible with a brush and a bucket. But making your own spray paint with a compression sprayer (following the instructions on page 24) will make transferring stencils and other artwork to the wall a cinch. Simply create a template with contact paper, secure it to the wall, firmly run your fingers along all sides for a firm hold and to remove any bubbles, and paint.

8 HARDWARE

Spray painting hardware might be the easiest possible way to renovate a room. With just a couple of bucks and an afternoon, your kitchen, bathroom, or dresser could have a whole new feel with the addition of matte-metallic-painted hardware.

floral drink corks

SKILL LEVEL: Beginner
TIME NEEDED: 30 minutes

Corkscrew flowers are the perfect way to brighten up a beverage cart. The painted corks will top glass bottles nicely and bring a festive touch to your home. They look especially sweet en masse at a large gathering, on a wine bar, or topping vintage Coke bottles. They also make for wonderful hostess gifts (along with a bottle of wine, of course). Use a cork from that pile you've been saving for . . . reasons you can't remember. Don't have a cork? Go buy a bottle of wine and enjoy that first!

Wine cork

White silk or plastic flower, 1 to 3" (2.5 to 8 cm)
    in diameter

Paring knife (optional)

Masking tape

Craft scissors

Wood glue

Waxed paper

Milk paint in color of your choice
    (purchased or homemade; see page 26)

Water spray bottle

Skim milk

INSTRUCTIONS

❶ Wash the cork and flower thoroughly and set them aside
to dry.

❷ If you'd like, test your cork to see how it fits into the bottle
you plan to use. If necessary, pare the cork down with a knife
for a perfectly secure fit.

❸ Tape around the sides of the cork with masking tape. Next,
carve a small hole in the top of the cork by carefully twisting
the sharp end of a pair of scissors into it.

❹ Remove the artificial flower head from its branch, leaving
a length of stem about 1½" (4 cm). Dab a bit of wood glue
on the end of the stem and gently twist it into the hole you
made in the cork.

❺ Set the flowered cork on a work surface covered with waxed
paper. Pour the milk paint into the water spray bottle. Test
the paint spray—if it is not spraying properly, thin the paint
with a small amount of skim milk.

❻ Spray the cork and flower with milk paint to cover. Set aside
to dry completely before using. After drying, remove the
masking tape from the cork.

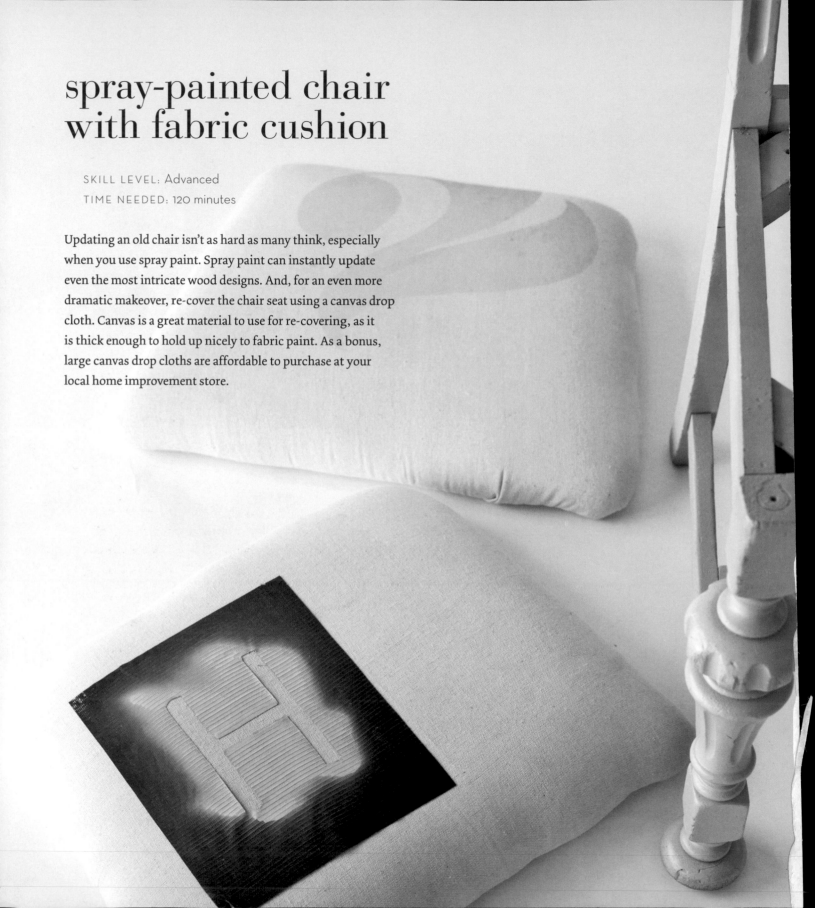

spray-painted chair
with fabric cushion

SKILL LEVEL: Advanced
TIME NEEDED: 120 minutes

Updating an old chair isn't as hard as many think, especially
when you use spray paint. Spray paint can instantly update
even the most intricate wood designs. And, for an even more
dramatic makeover, re-cover the chair seat using a canvas drop
cloth. Canvas is a great material to use for re-covering, as it
is thick enough to hold up nicely to fabric paint. As a bonus,
large canvas drop cloths are affordable to purchase at your
local home improvement store.

SUPPLIES

An old chair with a fabric-covered seat
  (mine was thrifted)
Screwdriver or power drill
Sandpaper (optional)
Spray primer in gray
Spray paint in color of your choice
Canvas drop cloth (optional)
Staple gun (optional)
Painter's tape
Plastic stencils (see note)
Fabric paint
Compression sprayer (see page 24)

NOTE: *I used a 10" (25-cm) Helvetica and 12" (30.5-cm) brushfont stencil for this project.*

INSTRUCTIONS

❶ Turn the chair over and unscrew all of the bottom screws with a screwdriver or power drill. Remove the cushioned seat and set it aside.

❷ Lightly sand the entire chair with sandpaper, then wipe clean and coat with one layer of gray spray primer. I like using gray rather than white for a more vintage look. (If you use a darker primer you can skip the tedious sanding process unless there are heavy imperfections in the wood.) Once fully dry, add one to two coats of your favorite spray paint, waiting for each layer to dry before beginning another.

❸ If you'd like, you can re-cover the cushioned seat using the canvas drop cloth. If you're familiar with reupholstering, go ahead and disassemble the entire seat, replacing the stuffing if you'd like. If not, just place the chair seat as-is, covered side down, on your canvas. Working around the edge of the seat, pull the canvas taut over the edge of the seat onto the bottom side and use a staple gun to attach the canvas to the bottom of the cushion.

❹ Tape your stencil squarely on the fabric of the chair seat. If necessary, cover any exposed areas of the seat with additional painter's tape.

❺ Thin your fabric paint with a bit of water, and pour it into your compression sprayer. Spray directly onto the seat, keeping within the stencil. Let dry completely before removing the stencil.

❻ Screw the seat cushion back to the chair base and enjoy the gorgeous update to your dining room.

metal can storage bins

SKILL LEVEL: Intermediate
TIME NEEDED: 90 minutes

There are many storage solutions available today, the majority of which could use a vibrant pick-me-up. Instead of investing in a storage unit that may not work for your space, make one that doubles as an art piece by combining a collection of mismatched tin cans and spray painting them to suit your style.

SUPPLIES

Metal cans of varying sizes
Can opener
File
Spray paint in the colors of
    your choice (I used two colors:
    one for the inside and one
    for the outside of the cans)
Painter's tape (mine was
    2" [5 cm] wide)
Spray primer in white
Pencil
One package of $\frac{1}{4}$" (6-mm) stove
    or machine nuts and bolts
Power drill with $\frac{1}{4}$" (6-mm)
    drill bit
Flat-head screwdriver
Adjustable wrench

INSTRUCTIONS

1. Use a can opener to remove one end of each metal can; file rough edges.

2. Spray paint the outside of the cans in the color of your choice. Pay attention to any grooves in the cans, and don't worry about getting paint on the inside. Set aside to dry.

3. Once the outer layer of paint is dry, wrap the outside of each can with painter's tape to completely cover.

4. Spray paint the inside of the cans with the white primer (this will make the color inside more vibrant). Set aside to dry completely. Once dry, spray paint over the primer with one to two coats of your desired color—bright colors will give the most "pop" to this project. Once dry, remove the painter's tape.

5. Before assembling, plan out how you want to arrange your cans. It might be helpful to draw a diagram.

6. Starting with the corner can, carefully drill a hole in the middle of the can. Following your diagram, place the next can opposite, and mark the hole with a pencil. Carefully drill a hole in the second can.

7. Attach the cans with a nut and bolt. Make sure to tighten the bolt enough that the cans stay in place, but loosely enough that you can take them apart later if you want to change up the arrangement.

8. Continue assembling your creation one can at a time. Depending on the height of the cans, you may need to join some of the cans with two bolts to make the attachment secure. Make sure you do not add holes to the areas of the outer cans which will be exposed.

9. Once you are happy with your design, tighten all the bolts with the screwdriver and wrench. Fill with wine bottles, kitchen supplies, or small collections.

more projects to try

1 Using poster board, veggies, and paint, these fun art prints are a great family project for the home. See the full tutorial at A SUBTLE REVELRY: HTTP://ASUBTLEREVELRY.COM/CELERY-STAMPED-ARTWORK

2 A touch of neon, or another bright color, instantly brightens up plain dishware. Jeanne updated hers by covering the pieces she wanted to leave white with a plastic bag and tape, and then spray painting the exposed handles. See the full tutorial at SHOP SWEET THINGS: HTTP://SHOPSWEETTHINGS.COM/LIVING/DIY-NEON-CLASSIC-POTTERY

3 Painting a tablecloth is a great way to freshen up your linens. I love the look of this graphic criss-cross pattern Tina from *A Traveling Mama* created for my site with fabric paint on a simple white tablecloth. See the full tutorial at A SUBTLE REVELRY: HTTP://ASUBTLEREVELRY.COM/GRAPHIC-PAINTED-TABLECLOTH

4 Spray painting stripes is an art form, I say, and this schoolhouse chair is absolutely perfect. The trick to a beautiful piece is spray painting one last base coat over the tape to prevent any bleeding between colors. See more of Michelle's tips and the full tutorial at 4 MEN 1 LADY: HTTP://WWW.4MEN1LADY.COM/HOW-TO-SPRAY-PAINT-SUCCESSFULLY/

5 Since we all know spray paint isn't the best for kids, creating your own batch of this kid-friendly finger paint using Lisa's recipe and dispensing it in a plastic spray bottle might just be the perfect solution. See the full tutorial at LITTLE MONSTER BABY: HTTP://WWW.LITTLEMONSTERBABY.COM/2012/07/EDIBLE-FINGERPAINT.HTML

6 Wicker baskets are an eyesore to me. They're plain, and they seem to multiply overnight! Cassie taped hers off in a pretty herringbone pattern and used spray paint to make it beautiful. See the full tutorial at HI SUGAR PLUM: HTTP://HISUGARPLUM.BLOGSPOT.COM/2013/02/DIY-HERRINGBONE-BASKET.HTML

plaster of paris

I LIKE TO THINK OF PLASTER OF PARIS as concrete in its favorite little black dress, out for drinks with the girls. Plaster of Paris is a mixture of gypsum and sand that forms a solid base when mixed with water. Working with plaster of Paris requires a process similar to working with concrete (mix the dry mixture with water and pour into a mold), but unlike concrete, it can be carved, sanded, and painted with ease. Plaster of Paris sets quickly, making it a fun material to use when you want quick results (especially when creating molds or artistic forms), and is readily available in most craft stores.

TIPS FOR WORKING WITH plaster of paris

1. Unmixed plaster of Paris is toxic, so be sure to wear a face mask and always work in a well-ventilated area.

2. Always use room temperature water to mix the plaster. If the water is too hot or cold, it will affect the time it takes for the plaster to set and could negatively alter the final project.

3. After adding the plaster of Paris to the water, let it sit for 1 to 2 minutes before mixing. This ensures that all the particles have time to absorb the water, making it less likely that you will have air bubbles in your finished project.

4. After the mold has been filled with the liquid plaster, use a rubber mallet or a hammer covered in tin foil to tap the sides swiftly to release any air bubbles that may have formed.

PLASTER-TO-WATER ratios

Although your plaster of Paris instructions will tell you there is one ratio, every project is actually a little different. By adjusting the plaster-to-water ratio (just a little!) you can achieve a firmer or softer finished piece. The artistic side of me is normally not one for incredibly specific instructions, but following these ratios really makes a difference in the end product. So try a few of them out as you experiment with this material, and watch your projects change in the most appealing of ways:

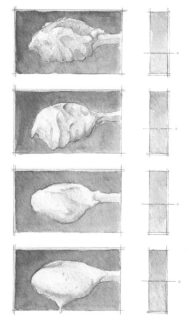

65% / 35% This should only be used for very large décor pieces and any plaster details that you will be adding to other materials.

60% / 40% This is a good, firm mixture for larger projects that will need to stand alone once cured.

55% / 45% A tad more plaster than water is a good, consistent mixture to use for most small home projects.

50% / 50% An equally balanced mixture tends to be a bit runny, but this mixture is the best form for adding in paint, as the paint actually works to harden the mixture more than water alone would.

plaster monograms

SKILL LEVEL: Intermediate
TIME NEEDED: 90 minutes

Nothing makes a home feel personalized like a monogram. I've included monograms and meaningful words all over our last couple of homes, and they instantly bring a sense of tradition and substance to the space. Plaster of Paris monograms immediately fit into any stylish décor scheme, but I especially love them set against exposed wood and brick.

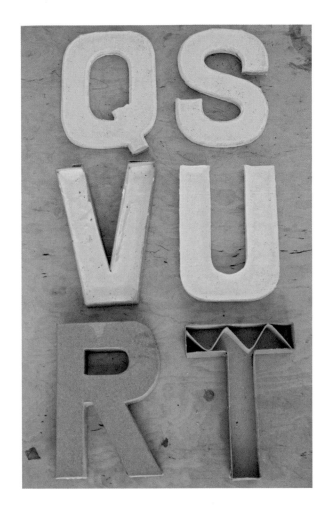

SUPPLIES

Cardboard letter molds (I used 12" [30.5-cm] ones)
Large mixing bowl
½ cup (63 g) plaster of Paris, per letter
Water
Old wooden kitchen spoon for mixing
   (do not use again for food)
Rubber mallet or hammer with foil-covered head
Hand sander or nail file (optional)

INSTRUCTIONS

❶ Start by opening the backs of the cardboard letter molds and taking out any inside filling. Thanks to mass production, the back of each letter will come off fairly easily. Since the part of the monogram that butts up to the cardboard is the smoothest, you will want this to be the front. With this in mind, your molds should be a mirror image of the letters you hope to produce.

❷ Because the plaster sets up very quickly, it's recommended you make just one letter at a time. In a large bowl, combine ½ cup (63 g) plaster with ⅓ cup (75 ml) water and mix with a wooden spoon.

❸ Pour the plaster mixture into your mold and tap the sides swiftly with a mallet to remove any air bubbles.

❹ Let dry for 24 to 48 hours. Once the plaster is completely set, removing the mold is easy: Simply peel off the cardboard. If any stubborn pieces remain after peeling off the mold, use a small hand sander (or nail file) to remove them.

FOR THE LOVE OF TYPE

I am absolutely in love with the resurgence of typography in design. Creative new digital typefaces pop up daily, and using an assortment of lettering on my craft projects makes them more personal and meaningful, as in the Plaster Monograms on page 41. Here are some other ways I like to use handlettering and typography in my own life and work.

❶ Adding lettering to white cotton pillowcases with fabric markers brings sweet secrets to life in any room. The set I currently have on my bed features a short meaningful poem.

❷ Writing a note of congrats, birthday wishes, or thanks on a plain length of wrapping paper (or even a paper bag) with a charcoal pencil will instantly turn an unadorned package into a custom-wrapped work of art.

❸ Leaving secret text on lampshades is one of my favorite tricks. Write words on the inside of a dark-colored drum lampshade with a black marker (be sure to write your words backward so they face out correctly) and watch the words appear when the lamp is turned on. Such a fun trick!

❹ Use a combination of corn syrup and sprinkles to quickly gussy up any glass for a spontaneous party. You can use stencils for perfect letters, or hand-script for a more natural feel. To make your own, write out your desired text directly on the glass with the end of a cotton swab (cotton removed) or a small paintbrush dipped in corn syrup. Then, sprinkle baking glitter or sprinkles

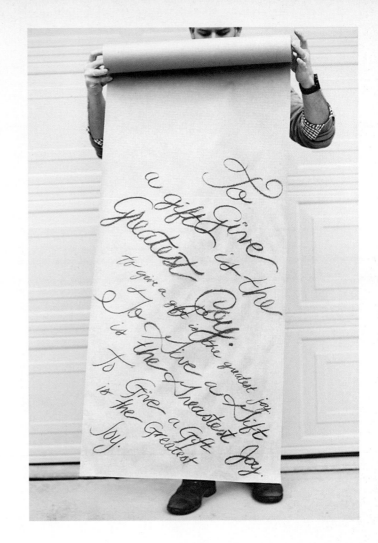

over the letters and allow to dry for an hour before drinking out of the glasses. The best part: the embellishment washes right off after the party!

❺ Writing on balloons is another way to make festive elements a bit more personal. Begin by filling up a rubber balloon with helium (I love the idea of a huge balloon!), then use a chalk ink marker to write a special message.

plaster painted chalk

SKILL LEVEL: Beginner
TIME NEEDED: 30 minutes

You could go to the store and purchase chalk, but it is much more fun to make it at home! With plaster of Paris, you can make chalk in any color imaginable, and it's perfect for writing your favorite words on a chalkboard or leaving a sweet love note on the sidewalk outside. For shaped chalk, use a pliable silicone ice cube tray in whatever shape you desire. For thicker, cylindrical chalk, use empty toilet paper rolls, wrapping paper rolls, or other hollow cylindrical molds.

SUPPLIES

Large mixing bowl

2 to 3 cups (252 to 378 g) plaster of Paris

Water

Tempera paint in your colors of choice

Old wooden kitchen spoon for mixing
   (not to be used again for food)

Small plastic bags, such as sandwich bags

Craft scissors

Molds, such as a silicone ice cube tray
   or empty toilet paper roll

INSTRUCTIONS

1 In a bowl, combine 50% plaster of Paris with
25% water and 25% tempera paint. Stir well
with a wooden spoon. Add in additional paint
to reach your desired hue.

2 Spoon the mixture into a plastic bag and snip
off one corner with scissors.

3 Gently squeeze the mixture into the molds. Tap
the molds on the countertop to remove any air
bubbles and set aside on a flat surface to dry.

4 After about 4 hours, carefully remove the chalk
from the molds and let sit for 24 hours before using.

3 WAYS TO MAKE A PARTY FESTIVE WITH CHALK

1 MAKE A CHALK PHOTO PROP

Nothing beats a photo booth at a party to get guests
engaged and having fun. Instead of creating an upright
one, try coloring a scene on the back deck for guests to
take photos horizontally! Leave out a bucket of chalk with
a few printed templates to encourage guests to draw. A
parrot on a shoulder, a chalked hat on a head, a stenciled
sword in hand . . . your imagination is your limit.

2 GIVE DIRECTION

Hosting a BBQ or block party? Instead of sticking signs
to a post or the ground, simply draw the directions on
the sidewalk. Phrases like *out back*, *almost there*, or a big
pink arrow will be sure to show your guests the way.

3 LABEL EVERYTHING

Chalk is great to use for party labels, and it gives
everyday objects some erasable flair. Try writing
guest's names on a their paper cups or using chalk to
label a selection of food directly on a wooden table.
Even seating cards can get a festive update with chalk
accents on the sides of plates or the edges of fabric
napkins to show guests their seats.

plaster pushpins

SKILL LEVEL: Intermediate
TIME NEEDED: 45 minutes

Making fun, personalized pushpins is a great way to kick-start your organizational goals. I like to make mine with number molds to help me remember dates and times as I stick reminders up on the walls.

INSTRUCTIONS

1. Line a baking sheet with waxed paper and arrange the cookie cutters on top. Remember to set the numbers backward, so the finished numbers end up facing the right direction.

2. In a bowl, combine 55% plaster of Paris with 45% water and stir with a wooden spoon to combine. Scoop the mixture into a plastic bag and snip off one corner with scissors.

3. Gently squeeze the mixture into the cookie cutters, cleaning up any side mess as you go with a damp paper towel.

4. While the plaster is still wet, gently push the blunt end of one pushpin into each cookie cutter until all but the needle is covered.

5. Let dry completely, and then gently scrape or sand off any remaining plaster from the sides of the pins with sandpaper. (Leave the plaster in the cookie cutter mold to give the pushpins a metallic edge.)

6. Poke the pins into cork, wood, or canvas, and get organized!

SUPPLIES

Baking sheet
Waxed paper
Very small metal molds (I used number and
  letter cookie cutters)
Large mixing bowl
Plaster of Paris
Water
Old wooden kitchen spoon for mixing
  (do not use again for food)
Small plastic bags, such as sandwich bags
Craft scissors
Damp paper towel
Pushpins
Sandpaper

more projects to try

❶ These plaster-laid doilies can be used for so many
great purposes like decorative bowls, tea light holders,
or hung in multiples as a wall display! All you have
to do is dredge your doilies in plaster of Paris and dry
them on an overturned bowl for shape. See the full
tutorial at FRESHLY FOUND: HTTP://FRESHLYFOUND.
BLOGSPOT.COM/2011/08/GENTEEL-AND-AFFORDABLE.HTML

❷ The best thing about these charming votives is the
price—only around $.20 a piece! Make your own with
plaster of Paris, a silicone mold, and a few tealights.
See the full tutorial at PAPER & STITCH: HTTP://WWW.
PAPERNSTITCHBLOG.COM/2013/05/08/MAKE-THIS-
MODERN-DIY-CANDLE-VOTIVES-ON-A-BUDGET/

❸ Creating a game worthy of a lazy Saturday afternoon
is a cinch with plaster of Paris and silicone molds.
Fill each with a plaster and water mix, paint your
dried pieces with acrylic paint, and start the fun!
See the full tutorial at SUZY'S SITCOM: HTTP://
SUZYSSITCOM.COM/2011/08/FEATURE-FRIDAY-BUG-
PARTY-TIC-TAC-TOE.HTML

❹ Making your own version of chalkboard paint is
easy by mixing plaster of Paris and an acrylic paint
of your choosing. See the full tutorial at A SUBTLE
REVELRY: HTTP://ASUBTLEREVELRY.COM/CHALKBOARD-
FLAGS

❺ These plaster-covered leaves are the perfect addition
to any dining room table. A tip: use fake leaves, as
they hold up so much better than real ones. See the
full tutorial at COTTAGE AT THE CROSSROADS: HTTP://
COTTAGEATTHECROSSROADS.COM/HOW-TO-MAKE-
PLASTER-LEAVES/

concrete

CONCRETE AS A MATERIAL IS MESSY and difficult to mix. But it is also one of the most fun materials to craft with, because it can create form and structure like nothing else. It is one of the most affordable materials to purchase (you can often find a 20-pound bag for less than $5!), and the number of projects that you can make just by adding water and pouring your mixture into various molds is astounding.

Although the terms *concrete* and *cement* are often used interchangeably in crafting and blogging, they are actually two separate materials. Much like a cake includes flour, cement is an ingredient in concrete, which is a mixture of four separate ingredients: rock and sand (70%), air (5%), water (15%), and cement (10%). The bag you want to buy from your supply store should say "fine concrete mix."

IMPORTANT TIPS FOR working with concrete

① PROTECT YOURSELF

Often DIY instructions will say, "wear gloves," but nine out of ten times I ignore this caution. Never with concrete! This material is not only toxic, but it will crust on your skin and do a number to your nails and new sandals. Be prepared—always wear gloves, an old pair of boots, and a face mask when handling any concrete, and if you do get any on your skin, be sure to wash quickly!

② COVER YOUR SURFACES

Floors, counters . . . it seems concrete can be made to look beautiful anywhere! But if you're working on a surface that you don't want covered in concrete, like your grandma's favorite tabletop or your newly laid wood floors, there's a danger that your wet concrete will stain those surfaces. Be sure to use a drop cloth with moisture protection under any project, no matter how small! I've also found a foam board works wonders to protect surfaces from staining while your DIY project dries.

③ PREPARE YOUR MOLDS

Concrete can be messy to work with and difficult to remove from the boxes or plastic containers I use for molds. Before you start, spray the inside of any molds with oil or a cooking spray for easy removal later.

④ POUR SLOWLY

When pouring concrete into a mold, it's important to try to eliminate some of the bubbles that will inevitably form in your mixture. Always pour slowly to avoid introducing more air to the mixture, and, once the concrete is poured, tap the sides of your mold with your hands or a hammer to force any remaining bubbles to pop.

⑤ ALWAYS LEVEL

When concrete settles and dries, it does so unevenly. Attempting to sand it down once dry can be challenging, so the best option is to level the project out as you go. Take a firm, straight level (if you do not have a metal one, you can use anything from a yard stick to a dust pan edge) and use it to tamp down the mixture every hour or so during the drying process to level out the concrete as it dries.

FOUR THINGS YOU DIDN'T KNOW YOU COULD MAKE WITH CONCRETE

Concrete is messy and strong-smelling at times, for sure. But it's such a fun material to work with for a relatively small investment. Once you get the basic mixing down, why not try one of these four awesome and unexpected projects?

❶ A BONFIRE PIT!

Fill small cardboard boxes with concrete. When dry, tear away the cardbard. Arrange the concrete rectangles in a ring that will work perfectly for keeping flames at bay.

❷ OFFICE DESK PAPERWEIGHT

Concrete is really heavy once it's dry, which makes it perfect for paperweights. Use an oiled cookie cutter secured to a foam board base to create a fun mold, and then pour in the concrete. Once it's dry, gently slip it out of the mold, paint it, and finish it off with a food-safe wax that will keep it looking shiny and nice on any office desk.

❸ UPDATED HOUSE NUMBERS

If the front of your house is looking a little bland, concrete can come to the rescue fast! Purchase cardboard mold numbers at your local craft store and fill with concrete (like the Plaster Monograms on page 43) to create your personalized street number. The numbers would look great glued to the front of the house with marine epoxy, or laid out in the yard to lead your guests to the right place.

❹ AN OUTDOOR DRINK COOLER

Want something more design forward than the plain plastic cooler at home? Simply fill a small Styrofoam cooler with concrete and insert a smaller cardboard box filled with rocks (like the Large Concrete Planters on page 54) to secure a wide opening in the cooler. Rip away the box and the Styrofoam once the concrete is dry and attach wheels on the bottom using marine epoxy for an extra design punch.

large concrete planters

SKILL LEVEL: Advanced
TIME NEEDED: 180 minutes

Purchasing large planters can be costly, but making them yourself out of concrete is wonderfully affordable, and makes for an accent piece that is both natural and modern. Although this project is large in size and requires a well-ventilated work area to construct, the end result is worth it—it's fun to make a few of these to brighten up a boring corner of a room and to place around a deck. Or, use smaller boxes to create mini planters you can give away as gifts.

NOTE: *The final project is quite heavy to lift—you may need help moving it!*

SUPPLIES

Ruler or tape measure
Two cardboard boxes, one 1 to 2" (2.5 to 5 cm) smaller than the other
    (I used a 16 x 12 x 12" [40.5 x 30.5 x 30.5 cm] box as my outside box and a
    14 x 10 x 10" [35.5 x 25 x 25 cm] box as the inner for my planters)
Wire cutters
Length of chicken wire equal to the perimeter and height of the larger box
Plastic tarp for floor covering
Large plastic mixing tub or bin
One 40-lb. (18-kg) bag of fine concrete mix
Water
Old wooden spoon for mixing (do not use again for food)
Work gloves
Face mask
A few heavy bricks
Chopsticks or a small dowel (optional)
Sandpaper

INSTRUCTIONS

1. Measure the height and width of each side of the larger box. Using wire cutters, cut one piece of chicken wire for each side, sizing each piece to about 80 percent of the size of the side.

2. Cover your work surface and surrounding areas with a plastic tarp, as mixing concrete can get messy. In a large plastic tub, mix your concrete and water using an old wooden spoon according to the package instructions. Be sure to wear gloves and a mask.

3. Set the larger box on your covered work surface, making sure it is sitting flat. Begin to pour the concrete into the box, filling it 3 to 4" (7.5 to 10 cm).

4. Place the smaller box into the mixture and press down firmly. Place a brick or two in the box to hold it in position, then pour the rest of the concrete between the sides of the larger and smaller boxes.

5. Slide the chicken wire into the concrete between the two boxes on all four sides, and press down firmly so it is completely engulfed in the mixture (but not so much that is comes out the other side). The concrete bonds to the chicken wire and it will give all the sides extra support for standing straight.

6. If you require a planter with drainage, use chopsticks or a small dowel to poke a hole through both boxes and the bottom layer of concrete, leaving the chopsticks in place.

7. Set the planter in a cool, dry place and allow to dry for 5 to 7 days or until completely dry. If you have made drainage holes, remove the chopsticks or dowels when the concrete begins to dry, but is not fully set, 1 to 2 days.

8. Once the concrete has dried, carefully tear away the outer and inner boxes and gently sand down the top sides of the planter before filling it with dirt and plants.

concrete lace coasters

SKILL LEVEL: Beginner
TIME NEEDED: 40 minutes

Anyone can get their hands on a few cheesy, cheap coasters, which are fine for the corner bar or for one use at a big birthday bash. But finding something substantial and beautiful to rest your drinks on every day can be a bit more challenging. Making your own coasters out of durable concrete is a fabulous solution—you'll use these beauties for years! Make a stash to keep, or give them out in sets as hostess gifts.

Plastic drop cloth

Small plastic mixing tub or bin

One 1-lb. (0.5-kg) bag of fine concrete mix

Water

Old wooden spoon for mixing
  (do not use again for food)

Work gloves

Face mask

Four 6" (15-cm) cotton lace doilies

Four 4" (10-cm) small disposable pie tins

Craft scissors

NOTE: *These supplies make four standard coasters. Cotton doilies are easily found at a craft store or while thrifting!*

INSTRUCTIONS

1 Cover your work surface with a plastic drop cloth. In a plastic tub, mix the concrete and water using an old wooden spoon according to the package instructions. Be sure to wear gloves and a mask. You'll need about 3 cups of mixed, semi-wet concrete for this project—allow the concrete to harden for about 5 minutes before pouring.

2 Place a doily flat in the bottom of each pie tin. The doily should be large enough to cover the bottom and sides with a little overhang.

3 Gently pour 1 to 3" (2.5 to 7.5 cm) of concrete into each tin.

4 Fold the edges of the doily over so that the entire fabric piece is adhered to the concrete. Trim as needed.

5 Allow the concrete to dry for 2 to 3 days or until completely dry.

6 The coasters should come right out of the pie tins when dry. Set drinks on them and enjoy!

concrete cake stand

SKILL LEVEL: Intermediate
TIME NEEDED: 90 minutes

In design, pairing contrasting items allows each one to really pop, like the softness of frilly lace curtains set against the backdrop of a rustic metal bed. I personally love to use this theory when entertaining—serving up trendy cocktails in vintage goblets and presenting cakes on modern concrete cake stands! This cake stand is solid and ready to hold the special confections for all of the important moments in your life.

SUPPLIES

Plastic drop cloth

Craft scissors

Waxed paper

Circular cake or pie tin

Plastic mixing tub or bin

One 5-lb. (2-kg) bag of
    fine concrete mix

Water

Old wooden spoon for mixing
    (do not use again for food)

Work gloves

Face mask (optional)

Large plastic party cup
    (you know, the kind used
    for that game that rhymes
    with "Deer Tong")

Sandpaper

Concrete epoxy adhesive

Food-safe concrete sealant

INSTRUCTIONS

1. Cover your work surface with a plastic drop cloth.

2. Cut a piece of waxed paper to the size of your cake tin, and use it to line the tin for easy removal (no insert is required for the cup).

3. In a plastic tub, mix the concrete and water using an old wooden spoon according to the package instructions. Be sure to wear gloves and a mask.

4. Fill the plastic cup to the brim and the cake tin halfway with concrete.

5. Set aside and let dry for 24 to 48 hours or until completely dry. Remove the concrete cup form from the plastic cup and stand it upside down. Gently turn the cake tin over—the waxed paper liner should make it easy to remove the concrete form from the tin.

6. Sand down the base and top of the cup form and the concrete cake plate to make them even. Place a quarter-size dollop of concrete epoxy adhesive on the base of the cup form, and place the concrete cake plate directly on top of the base. Hold it in place for a couple of minutes to allow the epoxy to bond. Let the epoxy dry according to the manufacturer's instructions.

7. Finish off the top of the cake stand with a thin layer of penetrating food-safe concrete sealant to protect your cake.

FIVE EASY WAYS TO GUSSY UP A CAKE

Taking a basic cake recipe and making it something special is an art I've honed to a "T," a skill that comes in handy when you're a busy mom. Here are my five favorite ways to instantly gussy up a cake and make it look splendid on whatever cake stand you might be using (though I'm partial to the Concrete Cake Stand on page 58):

❶ Melt store-bought frosting in the microwave to smooth and soften it before icing the cake. Instead of messily globbing too-hard frosting onto your cake, gently drizzling a smooth, even layer will make any everyday cake a showstopper.

❷ Toss a handful of felt balls on top! Even though they're not edible, miniature felt balls will instantly turn any cake into a party-worthy dessert. Just be sure to remove them before eating!

❸ Dress the cake with candy. Revive any less-than-stellar frosting job by sticking rows of your favorite candy along the sides and/or top of your cake. I've done this with peppermints, bubblegum, candy hearts, and even frosted cranberries to make a cake really special. As a bonus, it gives your guests an extra treat to enjoy.

❹ Shimmer and shine. Purchase a jar of edible glitter at your local craft store and dust a bit over your cake to give it some sparkle. Even the most modest of confections will enjoy a boost of fancy with a few shakes of glitter. To ensure that the glitter sticks properly, dust it on before the frosting has completely set, or gently spray water on the frosting to make it just slightly sticky before shaking on the glitter.

❺ Write a surprise note inside a cake for a bit of birthday fun! Use edible dough (found in the baking section of your local craft store) and alphabet cookie cutters to cut out words to place inside a cake. Roll out the dough, cut out the letters, and stand the words up in your pan before pouring the cake batter on top. When the cake is cut open, the words will spell a sweet surprise for your guests.

more projects to try

HERE ARE MORE INSPIRING CONCRETE PROJECTS FROM MY OWN BLOG, *A SUBTLE REVELRY*, AS WELL AS SOME OF MY FAVORITE BLOGS:

❶ Gardens beds come to life with simple plant markers. Pour concrete mix into a simple plastic mold, stick a dowel into the center, and hold it closed with a zip tie to create these star stakes. See the full tutorial at CHEZ LARSSON: HTTP://WWW. CHEZLARSSON.COM/MYBLOG/2010/06/PANDURO-CONCRETE-CHALLENGE-5.HTML

❷ To create this simple concrete stepping stone that doubles as a planter, pour concrete mix into a large stone-shaped mold. Then, press a smaller mold in a fun shape into the concrete about halfway to make a perfect spot for planting seeds. See the full tutorial at TREE HOUSE KID AND CRAFT: HTTP:// TREEHOUSEKIDANDCRAFT-BLOG.COM/DIY/DIY-CONCRETE-STEPPING-STONE-PLANTER/

❸ Wondering how you can get a heavy concrete project to stay suspended in mid-air? Start with a plastic base! To make a similar lamp, coat a plastic or porcelain pendant with a couple thin layers of concrete. See the full tutorial at ESMERALDA'S BLOG: HTTP://ESMERALDAS.BELLABLOGIT.FI/ DIY-BETONIVALAISIN/

❹ Although these bedside lamps seem like an advanced project, this gorgeous design came together simply. First, connect the wood and metal pieces together. Then, set the concrete base with screws to easily secure the lamp once dry. See the full tutorial in the series of posts at NOMI DESIGN: HTTP://WWW. NIMIDESIGN.COM/DIY-BEDSIDE-LAMPS-FINISHED/

❺ Making a concrete bowl is as simple as pouring mixed concrete into a larger container and then placing a bowl inside to weight down an indention. Be sure to use a food-safe sealant if you will be using the bowl to hold ingestibles. See the full tutorial at A DAILY SOMETHING: HTTP://WWW. ADAILYSOMETHING.COM/2012/07/DIY-CONCRETE-BOWL.HTML

❻ This concrete project is substantial enough to center a coffee or dining table. To make your own, cast a concrete mix in a large mold and insert the candles as the concrete dries. See the full tutorial at MONSTERS CIRCUS: HTTP://MONSTERSCIRCUS. COM/2012/11/21/DIY-CONCRETE-CHRISTMAS/

paper

I TEND TO BE A BIT OF A CONTROL FREAK, so paper—which bends, folds, and changes with my every whim—is a material I love to work with. It's so easy to transform into something new! Good for everything from wedding décor to home renovation projects, it's no wonder paper is so beloved for crafting.

TIPS FOR CHOOSING *the right paper*

There are many different types of paper used for crafting, each with its own value, weight, and process. I've used many of them over the years and can tell you firsthand that it's easy to use the wrong type of paper for a project! Learn from my mistakes and get to know when you should choose which type of paper:

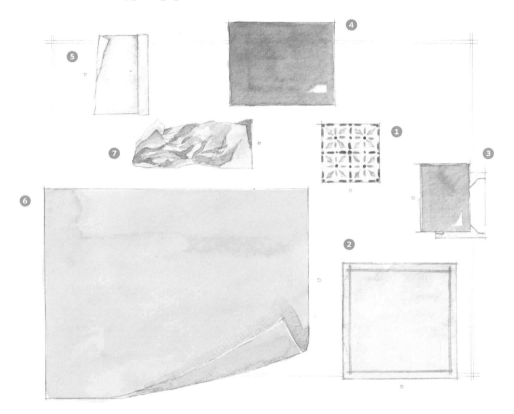

❶ ORIGAMI: The paper for folding! Origami paper can be folded into just about any shape imaginable. While origami projects take patience, origami paper provides the most options for creating original works of art.

❷ SCRAPBOOK: Thicker and often larger in size than other papers, scrapbook paper is my go-to for crafts of all kinds. It is easy to cut and comes in a seemingly limitless array of textures, colors, and patterns.

❸ MULTIPURPOSE: Multipurpose paper is most often used for printing projects and is the most affordable choice for any project. With its thin texture, the paper is great for tracing and papier-mâché projects as well.

4 **LETTERPRESS:** Letterpress paper is thick and has a gorgeous texture to it. Its heft is necessary to support letterpress indentations, but it is also a gorgeous choice for stamping and painting projects—it absorbs paint much like canvas.

5 **WRAPPING PAPER:** Wrapping paper is by far the best designed paper around. I routinely use it for stand-in table runners and for wrapping up pretty boxes around the house. Sold in rolls and priced anywhere from cheap to crazy expensive, it can bring an instant crafty boost to the home without much elbow grease.

6 **POSTER BOARD:** It's always a good thing to keep a stack of poster board on hand (and no, I don't complete third-grade science projects in my spare time). It's helpful for larger projects, as it folds and bends easily. Attached to two embroidery hoops it makes an impromptu pendant lamp (see Pendant Light with Tassels on page 88), and it can be useful for cutting forms for larger prints and designs. Stamping on poster board results in immediate large-form artwork to liven up any blank wall space.

7 **TISSUE PAPER:** The wispy nature of tissue paper makes it great for much more than wrapping. Use it to print decals (just tape it onto multipurpose paper and run it through the printer!) and apply them to your projects with Mod Podge in a decoupage style, or use it for papier-mâché or creating floral or fringe details on artwork at home.

DECORATING WITH PAPER AT HOME

One of the great things about paper is its ability to provide bright, modern touches in an affordable way. Decorating with paper is perfect for renters, too, since it is most often temporary (we move a lot, so I've gotten a lot of experience using this material!). Here are my favorite ways to brighten up my home with paper in 20 minutes or less.

MAKE A MOBILE. Use my accordion fold instructions on page 68, or make one with cut-out dots, triangles, or even lines of paper in a cascading arrangement.

CREATE A BRIGHT STRIPE. Layer strips of paper in your favorite color on a wall to form a bright, bold line. Use double-sided tape to hold the strips up, and they'll come back down in a cinch when needed.

LINE SHELVES. A simple solution for making an average bookshelf into something fabulous is adding color. Find scrapbook paper in a pretty pattern and use it to line or back your shelves. The custom look is a head turner and can brighten up a room quickly.

paper accordion mobile

SKILL LEVEL: Intermediate
TIME NEEDED: 90 to 120 minutes

Creating a paper mobile that will look great in any room of the house is easy with folded scrapbook paper. Whether making one for the nursery or to brighten up a reading nook, select bright paper for a whimsical design statement.

SUPPLIES

25 sheets of 12 x 12" (30.5 x 30.5 cm) scrapbook paper in coordinating colors

Rotary paper cutter

Ruler (optional)

Craft scissors

Hot glue gun

Hot glue sticks

Fishing wire for hanging

One ½" x 3' (12 mm x 1 m) wooden dowel for hanging

INSTRUCTIONS

1. Start by cutting the scrapbook paper into 2" (5-cm) -wide strips with a rotary paper cutter. You could also use a ruler and scissors, but it will take longer (a lot longer!).

2. Starting on one end, fold each paper strip crosswise using an accordion fold (below). Hot glue the ends together to form accordion circles.

3. Cut lengths of fishing wire, varying the lengths from about 8 to 24" (20 to 61 cm) for a full and organic-looking mobile. Gently thread one piece of fishing wire through the top of each circle and tie it to the dowel.

4. Once all 25 of the accordion circles are hung on the dowel, cut two 24" (61-cm) lengths of fishing wire and attach one to each end of the dowel for hanging.

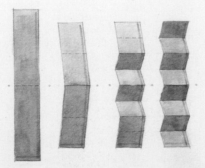

HOW TO MAKE AN ACCORDION FOLD

1. Fold a strip of paper in half horizontally.

2. Fold the paper in half a second time.

3. Continue folding until you have the number of creases you want.

4. Unfold the paper strip completely, then re-fold it along the creases, alternating forward and backward folds.

paper box lights

SKILL LEVEL: Intermediate
TIME NEEDED: 120 minutes

Brighten up a room or add color to the deck with these simple and festive origami paper lights. The translucent quality of origami paper allows the string lights to shine through, bringing a dose of happy to wherever they hang. Made with inexpensive supplies, they will liven up your home without breaking the bank.

SUPPLIES

One package of origami paper (usually
    sold in packs of 30 sheets at craft stores)
Length of white string lights

INSTRUCTIONS

❶ Make the origami boxes following the instructions opposite. It takes a little practice, so try a few and don't give up! Continue making boxes until you run out of paper or have made as many boxes as there are lights on your string of lights.

❷ Once the boxes are made, slip one box over each light, hang, and enjoy.

HOW TO MAKE AN ORIGAMI BOX

❶ Start with a square of origami paper; create creases by folding the paper in half width wise and joining each diagonal corner.

❷ Collapse the pre-folded base at the crease lines until you have what is called a balloon base or folded triangle.

❸ Fold each of the four corners upward to meet the tip of the triangle.

❹ Fold the four horizontal corners in toward the center so that the tips meet. Take the four loose vertical flaps and fold them down.

❺ Place each loose flap into the side paper pockets.

❻ Gently unfold the balloon center and blow into it to form the box shape.

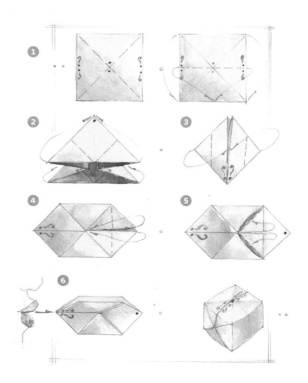

hand-painted temporary wallpaper

SKILL LEVEL: Advanced
TIME NEEDED: 120 minutes

Wallpaper doesn't have to be costly or permanent—creating a temporary version is easy using contact paper. The paper is sticky on the back and holds to most wall types well without any extra adhesive, and it comes down without leaving a residue. Contact paper can be purchased in many colors and textures and can be painted on. I love the look of my white paper with bright hand-painted arrows. Although I wanted my arrows to look a bit more imperfect, you can fill in your template entirely for crisper lines.

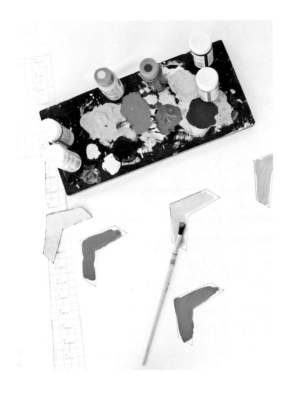

INSTRUCTIONS

❶ Measure out the wall space you'd like to cover and purchase contact paper in the correct measurements.

❷ To create hand-painted wallpaper, design a template or photocopy and then enlarge the template at right by 400%. Using a pencil, sketch or trace the template onto the contact paper in a pattern of your choosing. Templates with straight, clean lines are easiest to work with.

❸ Use acrylic paint to fill in the template. Repeat with the remaining rolls. Let dry for at least 24 hours (or until dry to the touch) before hanging.

❹ You will hang and line up the paper in a similar manner to regular wallpaper. Pull the backing off a small portion of the paper, and affix the sticky side to the top corner of your wall. Continue pulling off the backing as you smooth the paper down the wall (this part is best accomplished with a second pair of hands). When you reach the floor or the bottom of the wall, cut the contact paper roll with scissors or an X-Acto knife and start applying again at the top. Repeat with the remaining rolls, lining up the top and sides carefully, until the wall is filled.

SUPPLIES

Measuring tape
White contact paper (I used two 24' x 18" [7-m x 46-cm] rolls to cover a 10' [3-m] entry wall)
Pencil
Acrylic paint in assorted colors
Thick-bristle paintbrush
Craft scissors or X-Acto knife

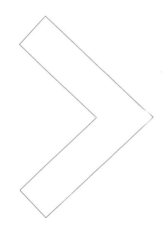

more projects to try

1 Decorative paper can update just about anything in your home—even the smallest detail, like a pencil. Cut into strips and gently glued into place, these paper-covered pencils are ready to make your office, desk, or kitchen a pretty lined success. See the full tutorial at HELLO HYDRANGEA: HTTP://WWW.HELLOHYDRANGEA.COM/2012/03/INSPIRED-BY-PAUL-JACKSON.HTML

2 This simple, bright paper artwork would make a major impact in your space. Cut strips of paper and curl each around a skewer, adding colors as you go. Once the circles are completed, a quick dip in acrylic sealant makes sure everything stays in place. See more images of this project at: HTTPS://WWW.FACEBOOK.COM/ICANCRAFTTHAT/PHOTOS_STREAM

3 These paper balls each take about a minute to make, and by combining strips of one piece of scrapbook paper with two staples, they are super affordable, too. Line a doorway, wall, or entire room with them for quick, simple, and pretty look. See the full tutorial at A SUBTLE REVELRY: HTTP://ASUBTLEREVELRY.COM/PRETTY-PAPER-PARTY-BALLS

4 Need a refresh for your table settings? You can create these wrapping-paper placemats in a flash! See the full tutorial at OLEANDER + PALM: HTTP://WWW.OLEANDERANDPALM.COM/2012/12/WRAPPING-PAPER-PLACEMATS.HTML?SPREF=FB

5 There is something so romantic about receiving fresh flowers in a paper bag. Create these adorable paper flower vases using a few markers and paper bags of your choice. See the full tutorial at A BUBBLY LIFE: HTTP://WWW.ABUBBLYLIFE.COM/2013/03/DIY-PAPER-BAG-FLOWER-VASE.HTML?M=1

6 Using a template designed by Chloé Fleury, you can make this simple cardstock wreath in a just one afternoon. See the full tutorial at THE PRETTY BLOG: HTTP://WWW.THEPRETTYBLOG.COM/STYLE-AND-HOME/PAPER-FLOWER-WREATH/

HOME
SWEET
HOME

thread

USING BRIGHTLY COLORED THREAD for crafting projects is one of my favorite ways to add boldness to dull spots in the house. Thread comes in a nearly limitless range of colors, and once you know the basics of working with this versatile material, you'll find that it's an easy way to update anything from fabric to wood to the artwork on your walls.

EMBROIDERY basics

Embroidery is one of my favorite crafts because the materials are affordable and readily available. I use embroidery floss for all thread-related projects when I can, simply because it comes in such a wide range of colors and it's incredibly easy to work with. For more heavy-duty projects you can also use thicker-stranded cotton thread.

I purchase and use basic embroidery (crewel) needles for all hand-embroidery and thread-related projects. Appropriate needle size is determined by the type of thread and fabric you are using: If the needle is too small you will have a hard time threading the eye of the needle, and pulling the thread through the fabric will be difficult. If the needle is too large the holes it leaves in the fabric will be noticeable, which can look sloppy. Always try to choose the smallest needle possible. When working with basic embroidery floss, I most often use a size 9 embroidery needle.

To thread the needle, pull about 15" (38 cm) of the floss through the needle eye hole. If you find you need more thread to complete your project, tie off and start again—too long of a tail can get tangled and will leave your project out of control on the underside.

To tie off a section, thread the needle back underneath the last stitch you made, leaving a loop of thread on the underside of the material. Thread the needle through this loop and pull to tighten. Cut the thread with scissors to end a line of stitching.

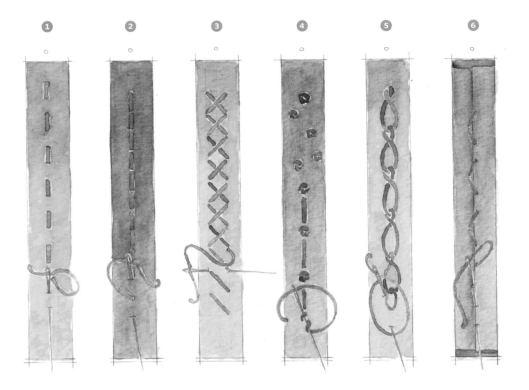

COMMON *stitches*

Knowing how to complete basic hand stitches will get you pretty far when crafting with thread. Here are a few stitches to get you started:

❶ STRAIGHT STITCH (RUNNING STITCH)

To make a straight stitch, bring the needle up through the bottom of your fabric and back down continually at even intervals to create a straight dashed line.

❷ BACKSTITCH

To create a backstitch, you will begin by making one straight stitch. Then, bring the needle back up through the fabric and instead of stitching forward, you will bring the needle back toward the end of the last stitch leaving very little space between stitches. This is good for creating a seemingly solid line.

❸ CROSS-STITCH

A cross-stitch is made by stitching on the diagonal and then running the needle under the fabric to come back up on the opposite diagonal, creating a line of Xs as you go.

❹ FRENCH KNOT (KNOTTED STITCH)

A French knot looks difficult, but it's really quite simple. Begin by pulling your thread up through the bottom of your fabric. Then, bring your needle in front of the thread line and wrap the thread around it twice. Once wrapped, stick the needle right next to the up-stitch hole and pull the thread tight before running the needle fully through the fabric. This stitch produces very pretty knots along the line.

❺ CHAIN STITCH

To make a chain stitch the easiest way possible, start with a small straight stitch. Bring the needle and thread back up about ½" (12 mm) down the line and run it through the first stitch, then back down through the original hole it came up from. Repeat by bringing the thread through the last loop every time to create a chain.

❻ SLIP STITCH

The slip stitch, used mostly to stitch two fabric pieces together, is a simple stitch to create. To sew the two fabrics together, gently slip the threaded needle through the very edge of one piece of fabric and then through the opposite piece with a diagonal pull.

PERSONALIZE WITH THREAD

Learning a few simple hand stitches seemed to open the floodgates for me creatively. All of a sudden I was walking around my house thinking of all the amazing things I could update, personalize, and make so much better with a little embroidery! And the awesome thing was that I didn't have to haul my sewing machine out, or invest a huge chunk of time in doing it. The process of embroidery moved from scary to exciting for me . . . and I may have quickly gone overboard! Here are thirteen things I personalized with hand embroidery that would be easy weekend updates for you to try as well. But take it from me—stop before you think about embroidering the sofa. It's not worth it.

1 NAPKINS. I added small hearts using a straight stitch along the edges of my linen napkins for a quick update.

2 LAMPSHADES. Adding straight-stitched lines in various colors gave nice texture to my lampshades.

3 PILLOWS. Backstitching phrases like *sleep tight* along the side of a pillow makes for such an inviting guest bed.

4 SLIPPERS. Bright, colorful French knot flowers make the edges of my slippers even brighter.

5 TABLECLOTH. We write the things we are thankful for over the years on our Thanksgiving tablecloth in washable marker, and I embroider over them before washing; the collection grows each and every year.

6 THRIFTY ARTWORK. Embroidered bow ties, hats, and pendants on a series of thrifted photos are perfect for creating a miniature art gallery at home.

7 BASKETS. Personalize affordable fabric storage baskets by spelling out what toys are being stored inside.

8 DRIED FLOWERS. Heartier specimens can withstand single straight-stitched lines on their edges.

9 MUSLIN BAGS. Embroider symbols that correspond to each kitchen supply stored inside on the front.

10 PAINTED WOODEN PEG BOARDS. Treat a pegboard as a piece of fabric, and use the holes to cross-stitch text, hearts, or flowers. This is a quick way to liven up a kid's playroom on a small budget.

11 STATIONERY. To give your cards an extra boost of sweetness, embroider your own little designs on them before sending them off.

12 ACCESSORIES. Adding a straight-stitched line to a castaway necklace or barrette will give it new life and a fresh color scheme.

13 SCREENS. Make window and door screens more crafty and fun by adding words like *hello*, *love*, and *smile* in embroidery thread.

french knot artwork

SKILL LEVEL: Intermediate
TIME NEEDED: 90 minutes

Using the French knot stitch and a basic template, you can create design-forward artwork in an afternoon. The texture of the French knot, combined with an ombré color palette, makes for a work of art that will draw the attention of your guests. I love the way it looks hung in a little entry enclave or above a guest bed.

SUPPLIES

Pencil
Plain white artists' canvas
Stencil (optional)
Embroidery thread, in varying hues
    of the same color
Embroidery (crewel) needle, size 9
Hanging wire

INSTRUCTIONS

❶ Sketch out your desired design in very light pencil on the canvas, using a stencil, if you'd like, or working freehand.

❷ Carefully consider where you'd like your colors to be (I started with the lightest thread at the top and worked my way down to the darkest). Beginning at the center of the canvas, create French knots (see page 81) in a varied configuration.

❸ Slowly move outward in your design, changing colors as you go. Once you are happy with your design, tie off your thread and erase any stray pencil markings on the canvas.

❹ Secure a length of hanging wire horizontally across the backside of your canvas, and hang.

backstitched wooden chair

SKILL LEVEL: Advanced
TIME NEEDED: 120 minutes

I am a huge fan of rustic wooden furniture, especially since you can often find great deals secondhand. With a power drill and a bit of thread, it's easy to update a wooden chair in need of some love to create a pretty statement piece for your home.

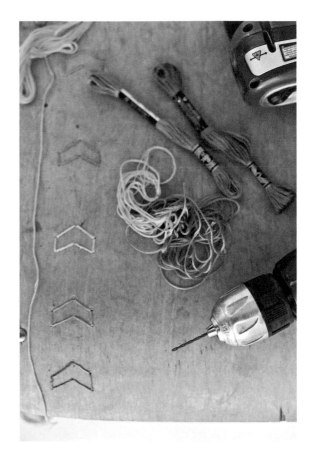

SUPPLIES

Wooden chair
Pencil
Power drill with a ¹⁄₁₆" (2-mm) drill bit
Embroidery (crewel) needle, size 9
Embroidery thread in colors of your choice
Acrylic sealant
Paintbrush

INSTRUCTIONS

❶ Start by sketching out your design on the seat of the chair in pencil. Geometric patterns with straight lines like the one I used are easiest to re-create with thread. Remove the seat, if possible, as it is easier to work with separately.

❷ Use a power drill to drill holes in the wood along your tracing lines. Make the holes at corners, where it is natural, and along any straight lines longer than 1" (2.5 cm).

❸ Thread your embroidery needle. Using a backstitch (see page 81), fill in the design outline fully.

❹ Tie off your thread. Use a paintbrush to apply a layer of acrylic sealant to the underside of the chair to ensure the stitches remain in place as the chair is used. Let dry completely before using the chair or reattaching the seat.

pendant light with tassels

SKILL LEVEL: Beginner
TIME NEEDED: 60 minutes

We've all had it happen to us: You move into a new place and there is always that one light fixture that looks as if it has been there since before the house was built. But you don't need to be an electrician to spruce up those old fixtures—rather than let them ruin the room, all you need is an hour and some crafting magic. Creating a pendant tassel light only involves a bit of poster board, some creative usage of thread, and some love. The best part: you can change out the colors of your tassels as the seasons change.

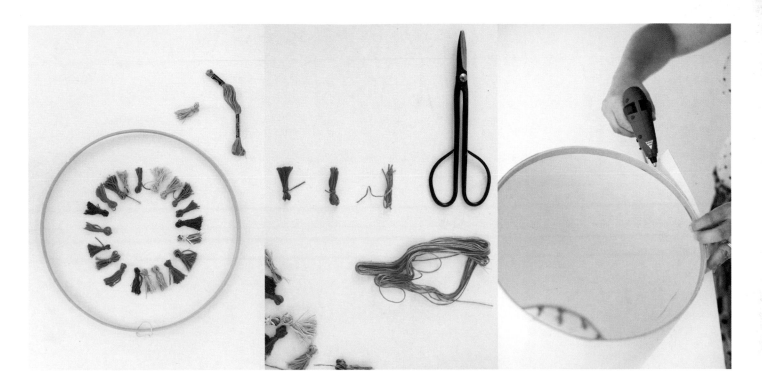

INSTRUCTIONS

1 Start by rolling the poster board into a cylinder to the circumference of the embroidery hoop, overlapping the ends. (You may have to use more than one sheet based on the size of your hoop.) Glue the paper around the embroidery hoop, and glue the side length of poster board together.

2 Wind a length of thread around three fingers about 30 times, until there is a nice thick bunch. Carefully remove the bunch from your fingers and tie it off ¼" (6 mm) from one end. Leaving the short loops intact, cut through the loops on the long end to create the tassel.

3 Hot glue the tassels along the bottom inside edge of the hoop at even intervals.

4 Glue the second embroidery hoop to the other side of the poster board.

5 Slide 4 or 5 S-hooks under the bottom edge of the pendant's top embroidery hoop. Hook to the current fixture.

6 If your new pendant is too wide to hook to the current fixture, or if you don't want to bother with the hooks, then use your glue gun to glue the pendant to the ceiling. Ours has been up for months now, lasting through summer, fall, and winter, and it is still firmly attached. I actually prefer this method as it gives a sleek modern look, but it will require a ceiling paint touch-up when the pendant is taken down.

SUPPLIES

One or two pieces of white poster board

Embroidery hoop large enough to fit over the light fixture you want to cover

Hot glue gun

Hot glue sticks

Embroidery thread in the colors of your choice

Craft scissors

Small S-hooks that fit over the light fixture (optional)

more projects to try

HERE ARE MORE INSPIRING THREAD PROJECTS FROM
SOME OF MY FAVORITE BLOGS:

❶ Add a pop of bright neon color to your home this year
with these easy-to-make thread-coiled bowls. Use cotton
jersey "yarn" made from strips of old T-shirts to create
a coiled base, and then loop neon thread throughout.
See the full tutorial at THE RED THREAD BLOG: HTTP://
WWW.THEREDTHREADBLOG.COM/MAKE-A-NEON-FABRIC-
COIL-BOWL

❷ Any material can be transformed instantly with a few
loops of colorful thread. To make this project, start with
a few unfinished wood ornaments and glue layers of
thread to your liking. See the full tutorial at URBAN
COMFORT: HTTP://URBANCOMFORT.TYPEPAD.COM/
URBAN_NEST/2012/12/DIY-THREAD-WOOD-CHRISTMAS-
ORNAMENTS.HTML

❸ An embroidered map is such a lovely way to decorate and
remember important places and people. To make your
own, check out our Embroidery Basics on page 80, and
take a look at the full tutorial at 3 SQUEEZES: HTTP://3-
SQUEEZES.BLOGSPOT.COM/2012/11/EMBROIDERED-USA.HTML

❹ Making thread rope bracelets is a great way to introduce
color to your personal style. These are made by wrapping
bright embroidery thread around a piece of rope and
finishing with some hardware touches. See the full
tutorial at WHY DON'T YOU MAKE ME: HTTP://WHYDONT
YOUMAKEME.COM/DIY-THREAD-WRAPPED-BRACELETS/

❺ Thread wrapped hangers are a lovely way to display
simple bulb holders. Thick jute rope is wrapped with
pops of colorful thread. Stagger the heights of your
bulbs to create a modern and colorful display. See the
full tutorial at A DOSE OF THE DELIGHTFUL: HTTP://WWW.
ADOSEOFTHEDELIGHTFUL.COM/BLOG/2013/07/DIY-THREAD-
WRAPPED-AIR-PLANT-HANGERS.HTML

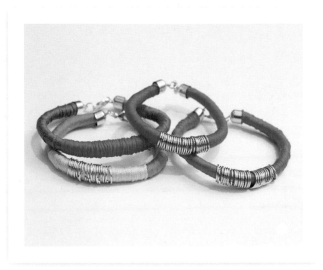

wax

WAX IS ONE OF THE STRANGEST MATERIALS to craft with. It has been around forever and has been used to sustain life, give light, propel many modern technologies forward, and depict creepy lifeless celebrity figures in museums. Yet, it is such a basic material—simply heat it up, and it becomes pliable and can be manipulated into a multitude of projects. As someone who values creativity, this fact alone gives wax a special place in my heart. With what other material could you boil a final product back down to its base and start again? There is beauty in that process for sure.

A PRIMER on wax

There are as many wax varieties as there are projects you could dream up, although the main types used in crafting at home are paraffin, beeswax, and soy wax. It is a good exercise to know all the different types of wax available and what they are used for. Here are a few interesting and often used waxes:

BEESWAX

Made from the wax that bees use in their honeycombs, beeswax is a natural wax material that is one of the easiest forms to begin working with. It is sold in slabs, natural bunches, and thin sheets perfect for candlemaking. The wax has such a low melting point that you can mold the thin sheets into candles using just the heat from your hands. This is great choice for beginners or for making candles with kids.

SOY WAX

Soy wax is made from the ever-loved soybean and is one of the newer waxes on the market (created in 1992). It is gaining popularity quickly because it is a renewable resource and burns clean. Soy wax is a great option for candles that are placed around the house, as they burn cleaner and longer than paraffin, and soy is also a renewable, biodegradable product. It is easy to use soy in conjunction with other natural materials like sand, bark, and pinecones.

LOW-MELT PARAFFIN WAX

This is the wax that you can find at the grocery store. It is used to seal jars during the canning process and can make gorgeous projects for the house (like the Wax Bud Vases on page 98). The wax has a low melting point and gives a pretty white layered effect when heated and dipped.

WAX CRYSTALS

Wax crystals arc a fun option for beginners. The wax comes in the form of small crystals and does not need to be melted into a solid wax form to burn. Stacked in containers, the crystals can be used to create a graphic display, or layered by color, they become a fun project to do with the whole family. You can purchase the crystals and pre-treated wicks at your local craft store.

JELLY WAX

With a texture that's true to its name, this wax is used in candlemaking and can be molded into fun forms for projects of various types. It is soft enough to allow for items to be placed inside the wax, like leaves, flowers, or small copper letters. It is a low-temperature wax that is good for beginners to work with, unlike its counterpart gel wax, which is high-melting and more dangerous to use.

MICROCRYSTALLINE WAX

This wax additive helps to harden wax and makes for more rigid shapes. It is often used for taper candles. I love using it to help form custom letter and number candles which are perfect for surprising favorite friends on their birthdays.

RECYCLED WAX

If you have candles, crayons, and other forms of wax around the house, making a batch of recycled wax is easy. Simply melt down any spare bits to create a brand-new material with which to begin creating. To get wax out of glass containers, stick the container in the freezer for a couple of hours and then use a butter knife to help lift out the frozen wax. Crafting at its most affordable—free!

POLYETHYLENE

This is the most used wax and it's made from the plastic in grocery bags and packaging. Before you go melting down your grocery bags though, be aware that this type of wax can only be safely manufactured by an industry professional. You will, however, use it at home if you are using molds of any kind with crafting wax.

FIVE ALTERNATIVES TO WAX CANDLES

Although candles like the ones on page 102 are our go-to for special occasions (or when the power goes out!), there are many other fun ways to create ambiance without wax. Here are a few of my top picks:

❶ Walnuts—or any oily nut—will burn. They look really pretty topping a carrot cake.

❷ Corks (must be 100% real cork) will sustain a flame when soaked in acetone alcohol for 48 hours first. Place a bunch in small taper holders to light up an outdoor buffet this summer.

❸ Any vegetable or fruit with a waxy stem (like an eggplant or cherry!) can become a small flaming

light. Use them beside a birthday cake for a wonderfully grown-up party vibe.

❹ When peeled, the pith of a clementine orange can sustain a vibrant flame for up to 20 minutes. Try replacing the orange's top once it is lit to make your very own tea lights—such a fun treat for dinner party guests.

❺ To create pretty oil lamps with limited ingredients, all you need is a mason jar, a 100% cotton wick, and a bit of olive oil. Fill the jar about a quarter of the way with the oil and punch a small hole in the lid with a hammer and nail. Push the wick through the hole about 2" (5 cm) and light it for a beautiful flame, no wax needed.

THREE WAYS TO dye wax with ease

❶ A number of natural ingredients will dye wax when heated. Try boiled and pureed beets for a purple color, cinnamon for a brown hue, or tumeric for a pink colored candle. An added bonus: your candle will burn pure and toxin-free with the added benefit of a natural smell.

❷ Using crayons to dye wax has become a wildly popular kid's project, and it's easy to do. Simply grate small pieces of two to three crayons, add them to your melted wax, and stir to combine fully. I often use five or six crayons to dye a small pot of wax. Don't wait until the wax begins to boil to start grating your crayons—it's a fire waiting to happen! Eeek.

❸ Artist pigment or wax pigment are great options for dyeing wax. If those are unavailable, concentrated food coloring in paste (not liquid) form will also work. Find it in the baking section at your local craft store.

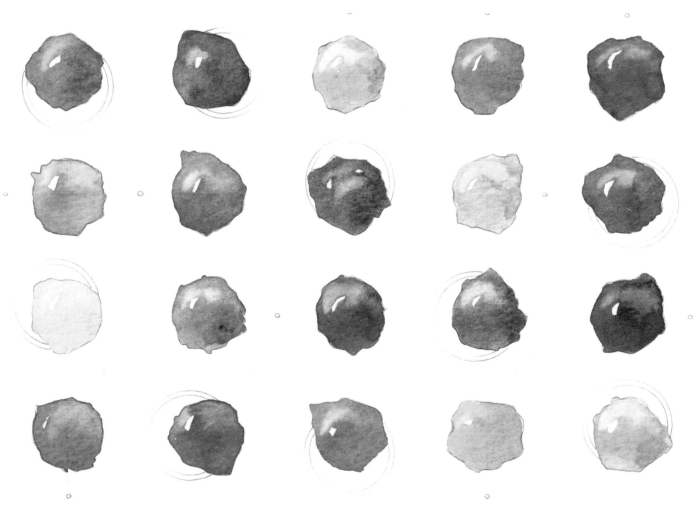

wax bud vases

SKILL LEVEL: Advanced
TIME NEEDED: 120 minutes

Paraffin wax is most notably used in the kitchen for canning or at the salon for skin-softening beauty treatments. The wax has a gorgeous translucent quality that makes it stand out as a delicate addition to the home when combined with a simple floral display. These bud vases are light and pretty, and their simple organic shapes make my kitchen seem calm on even the most hectic of days. Whether you make a batch for your own kitchen or make a couple to gift, be sure to try your hand at using paraffin wax—it's sure be soft afterward!

   The wax bud vases work best with air plants as they require no water. For a regular flower bud, put about 1" (2.5 cm) of cold (not warm) water in each vase; change water daily. The wax, though stiff in form, will warp if left near a heat source.

SUPPLIES

One small latex water balloon per vase

Water

Double boiler, or large saucepan and metal bowl
   (can be used again for food)

1-lb. (0.5-kg) box of low-melt paraffin wax (see note)

Paper towels

Craft scissors

NOTE: *Paraffin wax can be found in the kitchenwares section of most grocery stores, near the canning essentials.*

INSTRUCTIONS

❶ Start by filling a balloon a little more than halfway with warm water. Tie it off and set it aside, keeping it a good distance from the stove.

❷ In a double boiler, melt the slab of paraffin wax over medium heat. Alternatively, bring about 1" (2.5 cm) of water to a boil in a saucepan, then add the wax to a metal bowl and set the bowl over the pan of water, making sure the bottom of the bowl doesn't come in contact with the water.

❸ Once the wax has melted, remove the pot from the stove and let the wax cool until it has an almost white, creamy texture.

❹ Tilt the pan and gently swish the balloon into the wax once to coat it. Be careful not to touch the balloon to the pan (trust me—if it touches the pan, the results can be EXPLOSIVE!).

❺ Once the balloon has been coated, it is fine if it touches the pan. Dip the balloon into the wax 5 to 10 times to get a firm and solid wax build-up around the base.

❻ Place the balloon on a paper towel in a standing position to mold the bottom of the wax into a flat surface. The paraffin won't adhere to the paper towel, making it a great steady place to dry. Don't be too concerned about getting a perfect shape—the organic nature of the vase is part of its appeal.

❼ Let the wax-dipped balloon cool for at least 30 minutes, or until completely cooled. Pop the balloon at the top and pour out the water to release the balloon from the wax vase. Fill with flowers and enjoy!

wax-dripped cake toppers

SKILL LEVEL: Beginner
TIME NEEDED: 30 minutes

Topping a cake with wax doesn't always need to involve a flame! We love to bake cakes for lots of occasions when using birthday candles isn't ideal, like anniversaries, showers, or a good Thursday game night. These glitter-dripped cake toppers look like little lollipops just waiting to be presented. Keep a stash on hand for impromptu gatherings, and make your guests feel quite special walking in your door.

SUPPLIES

Saucepan (can be used again for food)

Water

Disposable 8" (20-cm) pie tin

¼-lb. (115-g) block of premium candle wax

Baking sheet

Waxed paper

Spoon

1 oz. (28 g) colorful fine glitter

Wooden or bamboo skewers

INSTRUCTIONS

❶ Fill the saucepan a quarter of the way up with water, and bring it to a boil. Place the pie tin on top of the saucepan. Hold the wax block in one hand and gently move it around the pie tin until a workable portion is melted.

❷ Line a baking sheet with waxed paper. Use a spoon to drip small dots of wax onto the waxed paper. While the wax is still liquid, sprinkle with glitter. Allow to dry for about 5 minutes.

❸ Place a skewer gently in the bottom portion of each wax dot, keeping the tip of the skewer within the boundary of the dot. Add a second drop of wax over this layer to secure the skewer and add strength to the dots.

❺ Allow each dot to dry for about 30 minutes or until completely dry. Gently pull the skewered dots off the waxed paper. Garnish cakes, treats, and other sweets with these festive toppers, but make sure to keep them out of reach of little ones who may be tempted to eat them!

colorful rolled tea lights

SKILL LEVEL: Beginner
TIME NEEDED: 30 minutes

Any excuse is a good excuse to make a day at home a special one, and these colorful rolled tea lights will brighten up a room in more ways than one. I love the vibrancy of colored beeswax, and these small candles almost look like confetti strewn about!

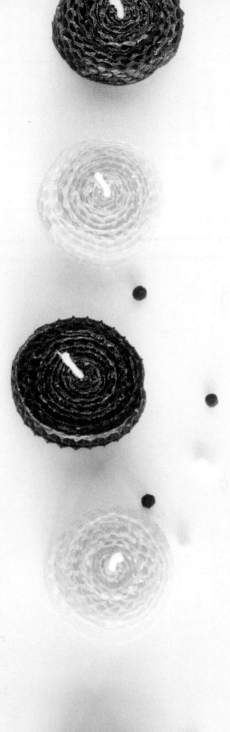

8 x 16" (20 x 40 cm) colorful
    beeswax sheets
Cotton tea-light wicks
X-Acto knife

INSTRUCTIONS

❶ Using an X-Acto knife, cut the beeswax sheets
into three 4 x 2" (10 x 5 cm) pieces per candle.

❷ Make the wax malleable by warming it up in your
hands for a moment. Overlap the short ends of
two of the pieces slightly and press together. Add
the third piece in the same manner to connect
the three pieces into one long skinny piece (about
11½ x 2" [29 x 5 cm] long).

❸ Press a tea-light wick into the wax at one end.
Starting from that end, gently roll the wax strip
tightly around the wick to form a spiral.

❹ Press the end of the roll into the candle base
to connect.

more projects to try

1 Wax is good for so many projects beyond candlemaking—you can use a thin layer of wax to create a waterproof effect on bags, jeans, and much more. Melt down a mix of paraffin and beeswax, then coat your fabric in thin layers before blast drying. See the full tutorial and more tips at TRANSIENT EXPRESSION: HTTP://TRANSIENTEXPRESSION.COM/DIY-WAXED-CANVAS-TOTE-BAG-TUTORIAL-PART-2/

2 Need an inexpensive handmade gift for a birthday or house warming present? These wooden spoons set the bar high, and conditioning the wood with wax makes all the difference. See the full tutorial at GOING HOME TO ROOST: HTTP://WWW.GOINGHOMETOROOST.COM/2013/DIY-CRAFT-PROJECTS/HAND-PAINTED-WOODEN-SPOONS/

3 You can't get any cooler (no pun intended) than these pinecone fire starters! Made from beeswax and pinecones, they'll get the party started for a camping trip deep in the woods or a bonfire on the beach. See the full tutorial at EVERMINE BLOG: HTTP://WWW.EVERMINE.COM/BLOG/PINECONE-FIRE-STARTER-FAVORS/

4 I've fallen head over heels for these wall hangings! Using a technique called "wax resist," you can paint your own designs with wax and dye the rest for your own custom creations. See the full tutorial at GOING HOME TO ROOST: HTTP://WWW.GOINGHOMETOROOST.COM/2013/DIY-CRAFT-PROJECTS/DIY-WAX-RESIST-DIP-DYED-WALL-HANGINGS/

5 Looking for a way to update your ho-hum wax candles at home? Use a decal made out of tissue paper to create an entirely new look in a pinch. See the full tutorial at JULEP: HTTP://WWW.MINTED.COM/JULEP/2013/03/21/FEATHER-DECAL-CANDLES/

wood

WHERE THERE IS A WOOD, there is a way! Hidden inside a tree can be a whittled toy, a bedframe, or an entire house— it is up to you to take this versatile, natural material and make it something beautiful and practical for your life.

WHAT YOU NEED TO KNOW about wood

To make simple crafts with wood, you don't have to be an expert in understanding wood grains or be prepared to bust out a saw at any given moment, although it is helpful to have some sandpaper and a decent saw handy. The key—purchase wood from a home improvement store that cuts the wood for you! Finding the right wood to work with is easy, if you can read between the lines (of the grain). Here are a few of the most common woods to use in your next project:

❶ **BAMBOO:** This wood naturally comes in tube form. As it is completely hollow, bamboo is a great wood to use for molds and candlemaking. It is quickly renewable, making it a perfect eco-friendly crafting option.

❷ **OAK:** Oak is like the classic J.Crew cardigan of the wood world. It has a pretty brown natural finish and a sturdy structure. I craft with oak when I want to build a piece that will last, both in substance and in style.

❸ BIRCH: Birch is one of the prettiest woods to work with. We have a birch tree in our backyard and I've often been tempted to just chop it down and start crafting! The texture and natural knots make it a perfect wood for decorative projects like centerpieces, bouquet holders, and picture frames.

❹ MAPLE: Maple is another great hardwood for household crafts. Perfect for those more substantial projects, it will last forever as a table or bed. Maple can be difficult to paint though, so I love it best with a finish of linseed oil (like my favorite shelves in our house). Why mess with nature, when nature is so pretty?

❺ PINE: Pine is possibly the easiest wood to use for beginner woodworking and carving projects. Pine is a soft wood that cuts easily and can be used for making toys and other decorative elements for around the house.

❻ CEDAR: Cedar is the best wood for outdoor projects! It has a gorgeous grain to it and weathers well, even when exposed to water. We use it for raised garden beds, birdhouses, and other fun projects to gussy up our deck.

❼ POPLAR: Poplar is a great wood to use for practicing the new techniques you'll be learning in this chapter! It is not terribly beautiful, but it is very affordable, making it a great trial-by-error wood for those new to cutting or burning wood. It can be painted easily so I often use it for projects that require a nice coat of paint to finish.

❽ REDWOOD: Redwood is another great wood for outdoor projects, or projects intended for the bathroom, because it is resistant to water. The redwood mat I made for our bathroom is becoming even more beautiful with moisture and time. This wood has a red hue that looks amazing when contrasted with slate or concrete.

TIPS FOR WOOD-GRAIN PAINTING

Paint is often the crafting equalizer—it can enhance nearly any project, regardless of the shape or style. However, there is a thin line between a gloopy paint job gone wrong and a gorgeous, thin coating that leaves the wood grain still visible. Here are a couple of tips to make sure your paint accentuates the wood you use and does not drown it in color and unwanted gloss:

❶ Always sand and prime any finished wood you plan to repaint. I've also seen lovely results from leaving the wood to cure outdoors for 1 to 3 weeks before sanding and painting for a rustic finish.

❷ Use very, very thin, long brush strokes. Try to cover the entire surface with one long stroke to give a uniform finish. Each stroke should be light enough that you should easily be able to see what is underneath it. Continue coating lightly until your desired color is reached.

❸ Paint along the grain of the wood. This allows the wood to absorb the paint better so the natural grain shines.

❹ You can also use linseed oil to finish wood. It's a great alternative to painting if you don't want colored wood, as it exemplifies the natural pattern and texture of the wood.

burned wood vases

SKILL LEVEL: Advanced
TIME NEEDED: 120 minutes

Woodburning is a technique that makes me want to put on a biker jacket and listen to "Beat It" by Michael Jackson. Something about the process of permanently marking a piece of nature with my own design is exhilarating, and with a simple $10 woodburning gun, it is totally possible for anyone to try it. These vases are a small-scale project that will introduce you to the process, but from here, the possibilities are endless: beds, decks . . . you name it. If it is wood, it can be designed and beautified by you.

SUPPLIES

Basic woodburning kit (find
    one at your local craft store)
Scrap wood
A small wooden vase (find one
    at your local craft store)
Pencil

INSTRUCTIONS

1. Before you begin to carve, replace the gun's default angle head with a pinpoint circle head and heat up the gun according to the manufacturer's directions. It is helpful to practice your technique on a smaller piece of scrap wood or the bottom of the vase before beginning your final design.

2. While the gun is heating up, gently sketch your design on the vase in pencil. You can print out your design and trace it, or freehand a design using a straight edge. Starting with a simple accent, like a star or oval, will build your confidence to create larger masterpieces—or go rogue with polka dots, organic arrows, or imperfect lines.

3. Using a firm and steady hand, begin following your pencil line with the tip of the gun, working along the wood grain for the smoothest break. Start by indenting a small line and then thicken as you go down into the wood. Try using your wrists instead of your full arm strength, as too deep a cut could quickly ruin your shape (or send you to the hospital!). Go over any uneven areas after the project is complete.

under-sofa game table

SKILL LEVEL: Intermediate
TIME NEEDED: 90 minutes

You can easily create a game board the entire family will love with just a simple piece of plywood and a bit of paint. Putting the board on casters makes for a great space-saving trick—hide it under the sofa when the games are over for the day.

SUPPLIES

One ⅜ x 24 x 24" (1 × 61 × 61 cm)
   square of plywood
Sandpaper
Primer (optional)
Paintbrush
Painter's tape
Ruler
Paint, in your desired color (see note)
4 casters (optional)
16 wood screws for casters (optional)
Electric screwdriver (optional)

NOTE: *I like to use chalkboard paint, as it allows you to keep score and write notes down as you play, but any kind of paint will work.*

INSTRUCTIONS

❶ Purchase a thin piece of plywood from your local hardware store. To get the appropriate dimensions for the project, ask for the wood to be cut there in the store. Most stores will give you 1 to 3 cuts for free on any wood you purchase.

❷ Sand any rough edges. If you want a cleaner finish, you can also use primer on the board. If using primer, let it dry completely before continuing with the project.

❸ Using painter's tape, measure and tape off a border 4" (10 cm) in from the edge of the square on all sides (or create your own pattern). Then, tape off a grid pattern to create the game board squares within the border. A standard checkerboard has sixty-four 2" (5-cm) squares (or 8 rows of 8 squares each).

❹ Paint every other square to create a checker-board. If using chalkboard paint, paint the border as well. Set aside to dry completely before removing the painter's tape.

❺ If you decide to add wheels, turn the board over and screw in small rolling casters in each of the four corners. No need to mark the placement or pre-drill.

PARTY GAMES

Rolling out the game table (see page 112) from under the sofa is perfect for a family afternoon at home. But what happens when all our friends show up? We still love to play games, but obviously need more room to enjoy the friendly banter and hilarity that comes from playing as a group. Here are three of my favorite party games to try out at your next gathering:

1 **BALLOON DARTS.** Lean a large piece of wood against a wall. Using a funnel, fill balloons with confetti, candy, and other fun party items before you inflate them, then tape them to the wood board in rows of five. Grab a set of darts and give each guest a turn to try to pop the balloons (blindfold them for extra fun!). Add a twist to the game by hiding a gift card or another fun present in one of the balloons.

2 **STARING CONTEST.** It might seem strange to start with, but everyone gets into this game quickly and ends up loving the awkward moments it creates. Pair up in twos and whoever is left will face off with the other winners, until there are only two left. The one who blinks last wins.

3 **CAMERA PHONE HOT POTATO.** Set your camera phone's photo timer for a minute or so, and begin passing the phone around the room. Each guest must pose for a photo, and pass the phone to the next person. Whoever is holding the phone when the timer goes off gets their beautiful "selfie" posted online.

rustic wood bunting

SKILL LEVEL: Beginner
TIME NEEDED: 30 minutes

You might not think it, but garland and bunting are not just for parties. I love
hanging strands of it up in our home for a festive and crafty effect in almost
any room. Does that scare you a little? While bright decorations would not look
out of place in my already colorful home, making bunting out of wood is an
easy way to bring in a festive element, even if you prefer a very natural palette.

SUPPLIES

Pencil

⅛ x 4 x 24" (3 mm x 10 x 61 cm) piece
   of thin basswood (find this in the
   wood section of your local craft store)

Ruler (optional)

Cutting mat

X-Acto knife

Fine-grit sandpaper

Waxed paper

Hot glue gun

Hot glue sticks

Bright colorful string or yarn, for hanging

INSTRUCTIONS

❶ Start by tracing a simple triangle shape onto the piece
of basswood. Make a paper template to trace, or use
a ruler for straight lines. Draw one triangle right side
up, and then another upside down to make the best
use of your wood. Draw as many triangles as will fit
on the basswood.

❷ Working on a cutting mat, use an X-Acto knife to
firmly press along your trace lines while holding the
wood in place. The wood should cut very easily. Sand
down any splintered edges for a clean finish.

❸ Once all the triangles are cut and sanded, arrange them
on a piece of waxed paper, spacing them as you'd like
them to be spaced when hung. Hot glue a piece of
string across the triangles, using a small dot of glue for
each triangle. Let dry, and hang as desired for a festive
home update.

more projects to try

1. Making your own batch of gorgeous wooden rings is not as difficult as it would seem. These rings are made by molding pieces of scrap wood with a large drill bit. Then it's just sawing, sanding, and finishing off the rings for a nice texture and feel. See the full tutorial at THE MERRY THOUGHT: HTTP:// THEMERRYTHOUGHT.COM/DIY/SIMPLE-WOODEN-RINGS/#_PG_ PIN=499076

2. By reusing pallets and adding in ledges, Brittany gave her wall an eclectic and organic look that will anchor the room for years to come. The process is simple, although time consuming, and involves carefully gluing, then nailing the pallets into the wall. See the full tutorial at PRETTY HANDY GIRL: HTTP://WWW.PRETTYHANDYGIRL.COM/2012/10/HOW-TO- INSTALL-A-SCRAP-WOOD-WALL.HTML

3. Using wood to redecorate an outdated desk is a fun (and beginner-friendly) way to get used to this material. This desk was made by attaching a pallet to the frame of an old desk. See the full tutorial over at THISTLEWOOD FARMS: HTTP://WWW.THISTLEWOODFARMS.COM/PALLET-TOP-DESK

4. Can you believe that just wood glue, a log, and a glass plate can be assembled to create a gorgeous cake stand worthy of your most delicious treats? See the full tutorial! at A DAILY SOMETHING: HTTP://WWW.ADAILYSOMETHING.COM/2012/01/ WINTRY-TABLESCAPE.HTML

5. Making these wood coasters is as easy as slicing up a log (just like you would bread!). Paint the coasters if you want a fresh, colorful look, or leave them plain and rustic. They make a great statement at home and are just perfect as gifts wrapped in twine. See the full tutorial on AT HOME IN LOVE: HTTP:// WWW.ATHOMEINLOVE.COM/EASY-DIY-WOOD-ROUND-COASTERS/

clay

USING CLAY TO CRAFT always brings me back to my childhood afternoons of working with Play-Doh, but now, as an adult, I use craft clay for a more refined result. There are a few different types of craft clay available on the market today, most of which are affordable and easy to work with (you can even make your own!). I love to make clay projects to add bright, crafty style to my home. Many of my favorite projects can even be done on a lunch break. So fire up that oven and let's make something pretty today!

THE BASICS of clay

There are two main types of craft clay with which you will need to familiarize yourself: air-dry and bakeable. Take a minute to review each before you get started.

AIR-DRY CLAY

Air-dry clay cures fully at room temperature in as little as a day for small projects, and a few days for larger ones. You can get a clean, professional look with this clay, and just about anyone, including your little ones, can have fun with it. It will shrink a bit, so make sure to take that into consideration as you plan your projects.

BAKEABLE CLAY

This clay has been popping up all over the crafting scene lately, and is fairly easy to manipulate into many creative projects. However, much like a cake, you have to be careful not to overbake or underbake the clay, to ensure the best shape and least brittle consistency. Bakeable clay lends itself to more customization, such as adding powders, pigments, and glitter to create special effects like mother of pearl, and it comes in many amazing colors. It is, however, a bit more expensive than air-dry clay.

The chart below lists baking times for clay $\frac{1}{4}$" (6 mm) thick baked at 275°F (135°c). The consistencies noted can be observed by pinching off a piece of scrap clay you can bake alongside your projects.

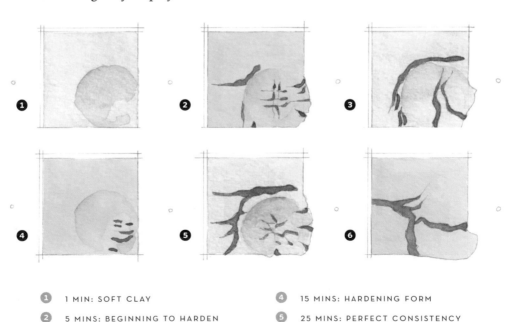

1. 1 MIN: SOFT CLAY
2. 5 MINS: BEGINNING TO HARDEN
3. 12 MINS: BAKING THROUGH
4. 15 MINS: HARDENING FORM
5. 25 MINS: PERFECT CONSISTENCY
6. 30 MINS: BREAKABLE & BRITTLE

MAKE YOUR OWN AIR-DRY CLAY

SUPPLIES

Large saucepan (can be
used again for food)
2 cups (240 g) cornstarch
4 cups (720 g) baking soda
2½ cups (600 ml) filtered water
Wooden spoon
Baking sheet
Waxed paper
Plastic bag

INSTRUCTIONS

In a large saucepan, combine the cornstarch,
baking soda, and water and heat over medium
heat, stirring occasionally, until the mixture
is about as thick as creamy mashed potatoes.
Once it reaches the right consistency, scoop
it onto a baking sheet lined with waxed paper
and let it cool to room temperature. Once it
has cooled, knead the clay for a few minutes
and store it in a plastic bag in the refrigerator
for future use. Don't wait too long, though—
it will dry out in just a few weeks.

colorful clay wall knobs

SKILL LEVEL: Beginner
TIME NEEDED: 60 minutes

Brighten up that entryway with these simple and bold clay wall knobs!
They add a touch of color that makes my comings and goings so much
happier, and they make it easy to keep purses and necklaces in perfect order.

INSTRUCTIONS

❶ Preheat the oven to the temperature indicated on the clay package.

❷ Divide the clay into 2-oz. (55-g) pieces. Roll each clay piece into a ball between your hands and smooth out the lumps by running your thumb around the outside. Each ball will be about 2" (5 cm) around.

❸ Gently twist the head of one screw into the back of each clay ball until only about 1" (2.5 cm) of the screw is still exposed. Gently pinch the clay around the opening where you inserted the screw to secure.

❹ Set the knobs in the baking pan on their sides, making sure the clay balls are not touching one another. Bake the clay according to the package directions. Remove from the oven and let cool completely on waxed paper. Allow the clay to cool on its side to keep the front round.

❺ Screw the knobs into the wall of your choosing for a perfect place to hang your things. You may need to pre-drill the holes in your wall, however, the clay is strong enough to hold the screws in place if you are able to screw them in without using a drill bit.

SUPPLIES

2 oz. (55 g) bakeable craft clay per knob

One #8 woodscrew, 2" (5 cm) long per knob

Small baking pan or pie tin

Waxed paper

Power drill with drill bit to fit your screws (optional)

clay antler mount

SKILL LEVEL: Advanced
TIME NEEDED: 180 minutes

Using clay for home décor projects often means you can get a huge bang for your buck and crafting time. This antler mount is a great example of that. Buying a stylish antler mount will cost you a pretty penny, but making it out of clay will just take an afternoon of crafting and some chump change. When designed in a bright, beautiful color, the piece can really work to tie together a room.

INSTRUCTIONS

❶ Attach the picture hanger to the back of your wooden mounting board according to the package instructions and set aside.

❷ Separate the clay into manageable sections and roll each out on the waxed paper. Shape each piece: create a head and then roll and piece the antler branches together a little at a time in an arrangement that is pleasing to you (I searched for photos of antlers online, and loosely followed their form to create mine). Be as symmetrical as you'd like.

❸ Stick the antlers to the head piece. Use your thumb to smooth out and strengthen any connection points.

❹ Use the remaining clay to cover the front and sides of the wooden mounting board, leaving the back exposed.

❺ Attach the head to the mount. Smooth out the connection points.

❻ Place the mount face-up onto a baking tray lined with waxed paper. You can rest parts of the antlers on cups and/or dowels to add dimension (otherwise, they will dry flat). Let the piece dry completely per package instructions. Once dry, remove from the forming cups.

❼ Hang on your wall according to hanging kit package instructions.

SUPPLIES

Picture hanging kit
Wooden mounting board
12 oz. (340 g) air-dry clay in the color of
    your choice (I am partial to bright pink!),
    plus about 2 oz. (55 g) for mounting
Baking tray
Waxed paper
Kitchen cups or wooden dowel
    (optional)

small clay bowls and vases

SKILL LEVEL: Intermediate
TIME NEEDED: 60 minutes

Making gorgeous clay pottery doesn't always require a fancy pottery wheel (à la *Ghost*—unless we're talking about date night!). Using air-dry clay, you can create simple mini-bowls and vases that are perfect for storing small succulents, candy, and trinkets. The great thing about using air-dry clay is that it does not require any special tools or the use of an oven, so it is an easy material for the whole family to enjoy.

SUPPLIES

4 oz. (115 g) of air-dry clay per bowl or vase
Rolling pin
Waxed paper
Bowls, cups, and/or vases to use as molds
X-Acto knife or dental floss
Foam brush (optional)
Waterproof varnish (optional)

INSTRUCTIONS

1 Roll out the air-dry clay with a rolling pin into a sheet approximately ½" (12 mm) thick. Air-dry clay tends to be a bit firmer than bakeable clay, so be sure to spend the time necessary to work it into a long, flat surface.

2 Cover your work surface with waxed paper. Turn the bowl or other vessel you are using as a mold upside down on your work surface. Lay the clay sheet on top. Gently press the clay along the sides of the mold, and trim any overhang with an X-Acto knife or dental floss to create a clean edge. Smooth out the lumps by running your thumbs along the outside of the bowls. Be sure to smooth out any creases or cracks to ensure the vases will hold water without leaking.

3 Let the clay-covered mold dry for 24 to 48 hours, or until it is solid to the touch.

4 Remove the clay from the molds and use your new clay vases and bowls for stashing beautiful things! If you plan to use the bowls as planters, use a foam brush to coat the inside with a light layer of waterproof varnish and allow to dry for 12 hours before filling with plants.

THE BEST PLANTS FOR DECORATING THE HOME

Placing plants in pretty pots around a room can add a subtle bit of natural charm to your décor. I'm partial to making my own planters (see Small Clay Bowls and Vases, opposite) and filling them with some of my favorite plants to liven up a dull room:

FIDDLE FIG TREE: The Fiddle Fig Tree has quickly become one of my favorite plants to have around the house. Ours looks a bit like a prop from a fairy tale, and I love embracing their whimsical appearance by potting these plants in oversize painted wicker pots. For more festive occasions, I like to brighten them up by tossing a small handful of bronze glitter on their leaves just before guests arrive.

SNAKE PLANT: We have a growing collection of snake plants in our home that lend their charm to our large dining table. The snake plant has gorgeous coloring and can grow with very little light, making it a great solution for creating an indoor garden for winter weather or rainy-day teas.

WHEATGRASS: Wheatgrass comes in wide, low trays and is a very affordable plant to have in abundance. It can run across any table as a centerpiece, and I even like to trim monograms into it for a special touch.

RED CLOVER: Red clovers are pretty *and* edible! Snip off a couple of flowers here and there to lend a fresh-from-the-garden touch to appetizers or desserts. Just be sure to wash them well before adding them to your dishes.

PRICKLY PEAR: The prickly pear is a cactus with pretty oval-shaped flowers that are edible. Prickly pear juice has a sweet and unique taste that is a perfect starter for margaritas.

more projects to try

HERE ARE MORE INSPIRING CLAY PROJECTS FROM MY OWN BLOG, *A SUBTLE REVELRY*, AS WELL AS SOME OF MY FAVORITE BLOGS:

❶ With bakeable craft clay, string, and an X-Acto knife for creating details, it's easy to make these tiny houses in batches for simple handmade presents. See more at A SUBTLE REVELRY: HTTP://ASUBTLEREVELRY.COM/CLAY-HOUSE-MOBILE

❷ I am always on the lookout for new and fun ways to personalize my gifts. Lo and behold, I stumbled upon these perfect gift tags you can make from polymer clay and a few paint pens! See the full tutorial at HOME-OLOGY: HTTP://WWW.HOMEOLOGYMODERNVINTAGE.COM/2013/12/POLYMER-CLAY-GIFT-TAGS.HTML

❸ Labeling drawers is a quick way to organize a room. This version only uses clay and craft stamps: make the pulls by rolling out clay or covering your existing drawer pulls (you can bake it right on!). See the full tutorial at LIZ MARIE BLOG: HTTP://WWW.LIZMARIEBLOG.COM/2013/07/DIY-CLAY-LABEL-KNOBS/

❹ Drawing on plain clay will give your project a whole new dimension—the color in this adorable hanging mobile isn't colored clay, but actually colored pencil! Use air-dry clay and a printable template to create your own. See the full tutorial over at CREATURE COMFORTS: HTTP://CREATURECOMFORTSBLOG.COM/HOME/2012/8/1/DIY-CLAY-NURSERY-MOBILE-OR-WALL-HANGING.HTML

❺ A great way to gussy up clay is by adding texture to it, and an X-Acto knife is the best tool for the job. Try adding pretty scallops to bakeable clay for your own personalized jewelry tray! See the full tutorial at FLOURISH AND HOPE: HTTP://FLOURISHANDHOPE.COM/DIY-CLAY-TRAY/

glue

GLUE IS A MAGIC-MAKER when it comes to craft projects. It combines, secures, and—depending on the type of glue material used—can transform seemingly simple, everyday items into something unique. Glue is what holds many of the things in our life together: Think about how often it is used in the architecture of your home, the construction of your furniture, or even this book. Why not trust it for your home décor crafts? Learning how to use the right kind of glue, and learning how to use it correctly, can completely change the way you craft at home. With a basket of different glues close at hand, you can take a simple idea and transform it into something beautiful.

WHAT GLUE IS BEST for your project?

With so many different types of glue on the shelves it can be hard to determine exactly which type will work appropriately with the materials you have. Here is the lowdown on the seven types of glue I find most effective for crafts of all types:

❶ SUPERGLUE

Superglue is the go-to glue for breaks, fixes, and securing items that nothing else will bond. Because of its instantaneous and permanent water-based bond, it works on any nonporous material that has traces of water in it—which is basically everything. It dries clear and should always be used with care because it is flammable, can irritate skin, and can be difficult to remove.

❷ HOT GLUE

The benefit of hot glue is all in its form. Using a solid glue stick and heating gun, hot glue can bond most lightweight projects in just seconds. It is my glue of choice for craft projects, and works great for securing art and small objects to walls and other surfaces. Hot glue is a good choice for stacking and combining materials that need an immediate bond.

❸ FABRIC GLUE

Fabric glue is perfect for fabric projects of most types. It is best for securing fabric to other materials and when creating multimedia textile-based projects. Many types of fabric glue are washable.

❹ WOOD GLUE

"Wood" glue is not just a clever name—it's the best choice for wood projects, providing a very solid hold after a couple of hours of dry time. The glue remains rubbery while setting, so the wood pieces need to be secured in place (normally with clamps) while they dry, which is something to consider before starting any wood-based project. An easy tip for small projects is to "clamp" the wood with a small length of masking tape and remove once the glue has set.

❺ ACRYLIC SEALANT

Most often sold under the name "Mod Podge," this glue is thin and has a water-based varnish added in production, allowing the glue to be applied to paper and thin-layer crafts. When dried, this glue not only bonds projects, but gives them a protective coating layer as well. The glue is most often applied with a small bristle or foam brush for larger areas, although I've found nothing works as well as using your thumb for smaller crafts.

❻ EPOXY GLUE

Epoxy glue has a strength and pliability that makes it great for adhering projects of all types. Use it to bond metals, plastic, wood, and many other materials. The dual bond makes it an especially great option for outdoor projects, as the substance can sustain many changes of environment. To get the strongest hold with epoxy glue, apply it liberally and allow a thick bond to form between the materials.

❼ SPRAY GLUE

Spray glue is a great alternative for projects needing a thin and consistent coating. Spraying allows small droplets of glue to cover a variety of surfaces with ease. Plus, the glue dries instantly. Spray glue does stick to anything in sight though, so be sure to cover any nearby surfaces and your hands well when using it (trust me, I've learned this the hard way).

MAKE YOUR OWN ACRYLIC SEALANT

Mod Podge is every crafter's first glue of choice because it is easy to use on a variety of projects to both bond and seal. It can be a costly glue to purchase though, so making your own is a good alternative for the beginner crafter.

SUPPLIES

12 oz. (360 ml) white crafting glue

6 oz. (180 ml) filtered water

2 tablespoons clear water-based varnish

16 oz. (480 ml) clean mason jar

INSTRUCTIONS

Mix the glue, water, and varnish together in a clean mason jar. Use as you would store-bought Mod Podge—applying a thin layer under and over your project for firm adhesion.

photo-print craft letters

SKILL LEVEL: Intermediate
TIME NEEDED: 60 minutes

If you are looking for a fun and modern way to display your recent family photo session, these photo-print letters are a great option. They showcase photos in a whimsical way that is less obtrusive on the mantel than, say, a huge mahogany frame.

INSTRUCTIONS

1. Determine how you want to position the photos on each cardboard craft letter, placing important photo details in a pleasing alignment. Mark the placement with a pencil and remove the photo.

2. Spread a thin layer of acrylic sealant with a small foam brush to cover the entire face of each craft letter.

3. Place the photo in the predetermined position, adhering it to the sealant. Smooth out any bubbles with your fingertips.

4. Cut each corner of the photo with scissors. Paint a layer of acrylic sealant along the sides of each craft letter, and firmly press the photo edges down over the sides.

5. Apply a second layer of sealant to the tops of the photos. Let dry and enjoy showcasing your family in a crafty new way.

TIP: *Use smaller prints to fill each letter for a collage effect.*

SUPPLIES

Several 8 x 10" (20 x 25 cm) prints
   of your favorite photos
Cardboard craft letters
Pencil
Acrylic sealant, homemade (see page
   135) or store-bought
Small foam brush
Craft scissors

THREE TIPS FOR REVELRY AT HOME

When you establish a home that is festive and bright, adding in updates for holidays and parties doesn't have to be difficult. In fact, it can be downright simple! Here are three tips I have for a seamless transition from every day to special day home décor:

❶ BRING IN BRIGHT ELEMENTS

My home has a lot of neutrals, which I like to break up with touches of bright colors. They liven up the everyday, and serve as a great starting point for celebration décor. If we are having a dinner party, my already festive polka dot tablecloth sets the mood without much fuss. If we are celebrating a birthday in the living room, the colorful confetti cloth makes for a great backdrop—no thumbtacks needed.

❷ USE GARLAND YEAR-ROUND

Many people think of bunting or garlands strictly as party décor—something you put up for a day and then take down. I see that as a waste of time and resources. Instead, invest in really pretty bunting or make creative décor (like the Rustic Wood Bunting on page 116 or the Tissue-Glued Artwork on page 142) that will look amazing every day. This will have you ready to celebrate at the drop of a hat.

❸ DON'T FORGET THE WINDOWS

Whenever we are throwing a party, I love hanging something pretty in the center of our windows, like the wreath from the front door, or one I have in storage. It doesn't cost a cent to move around and really makes a room look purposefully festive.

indoor clouds

SKILL LEVEL: Beginner
TIME NEEDED: 90 minutes

Every child loves to lie in the grass and watch the clouds move, hoping to spot a favorite animal floating by (who am I kidding—even *I* love to do this). Give a child the chance to imagine all their favorites every night with these whimsical, drifting batting clouds. These are also wonderful when grouped in an empty corner for every family member to enjoy.

SUPPLIES

Scissors

Medium to large cardboard box

Fishing wire cut in pieces 2 to 4' long
   (61 to 122 cm), depending on
      how long you want it to hang

Drop cloth

Plastic gloves

Protective glasses

Spray adhesive

1 bag loose polyester fiberfill per cloud

Thumbtacks, for hanging

TIP: *You don't have to purchase cardboard for this project. Try asking your favorite coffee shop if they'd be willing to part with a few boxes from this week's shipment for one of their favorite customers.*

INSTRUCTIONS

1 Cut down the cardboard box to your preferred cloud shapes (I made a mix of circular and animal shapes), using one side of the box for each cloud.

2 Make holes with the tip of your scissors and thread each cloud with fishing wire for hanging. To create the fluffy circular clouds, thread the string from the center of the cardboard. For animal shapes, be sure to thread on 2 or 3 sides to allow the clouds to hang upright.

3 Cover your work surface and surrounding area with a drop cloth. Wearing protective gloves and glasses, begin spraying the cardboard with the spray adhesive and placing small bunches of fiberfill all around the clouds. Continue in this manner until the entire cloud is covered. For more defined shapes (like a whale's tail), wait until the glue is dry and trim away the fiberfill along the edges of the cardboard shape.

4 Hang and enjoy. The clouds are so light that a simple thumbtack will keep them floating.

tissue-glued artwork

SKILL LEVEL: Advanced
TIME NEEDED: 120 minutes

One of the wonders of glue is its ability to transform an everyday object into one of substantial beauty. These tissue flowers are basic in nature, and pretty on their own, yet connected with a line of glue they become a show-stopping piece of art that will add a touch of style to any wall.

SUPPLIES

Tissue paper in assorted colors, cut into 8" (20-cm) squares
Stapler
Scissors
Hot glue gun
Hot glue sticks
1 spool 4-mm vine-covered floral wire
Wire cutters

INSTRUCTIONS

1. Make a stack of five tissue paper squares. Accordion fold (see page 68) the entire stack of tissue into one rectangle shape and staple it together in the center.

2. Snip the ends of the rectangle into a tapered shape. Carefully pull apart the layers of tissue paper to create a full flower shape.

3. Once you have created your desired number of flowers, turn them over and use hot glue to attach each one to a thick length of vine-covered floral wire at regular intervals. When you're happy with the length of your vine, trim the end from the spool with wire cutters.

4. Once the flowers are attached, twist and turn the wire as desired to create a gorgeous display that will liven up any wall at home.

more projects to try

❶ Glue is the obvious material of choice for projects that could use a little shimmer and shine. Use a clear sealant to ensure glitter stays where it was glued! See the full tutorial for these glitter hangers at A BUBBLY LIFE: HTTP://WWW.ABUBBLYLIFE. COM/2013/02/GLITTER-HANGERS-DIY-AVOID-GETTING.HTML

❷ This simple clutch is adorned with circles of hardened glue that are painted and threaded right onto the fabric. See the full tutorial at FABRIC PAPER GLUE: HTTP://WWW. FABRICPAPERGLUE.COM/2013/06/TRY-THIS-MOD-MELTS-EMBELLISHED-CLUTCH.HTML

❸ A thin layer of glue and a sprinkle of glitter makes this formerly ho-hum air plant holder into something to notice. See the full tutorial at 52 WEEKS PROJECT: HTTP://52WEEKS PROJECT.COM/POST/54872911208/GLITTER-DIPPED-AIR-PLANT-HOLDER

❹ Need that extra touch on your mantel or in your new workspace? This gentle reminder to "chill out" (which you can also replace with your favorite saying) made from a simple plastic tray, glue, and some spray paint is just the thing. See the full tutorial at FABRIC PAPER GLUE: HTTP://WWW.FABRICPAPERGLUE.COM/2014/01/TRY-THIS-INSPIRATIONAL-HEX-PLAQUE.HTML

❺ According to Aunt Peaches, we should never spend more than five minutes decorating a cake that everyone will spend less than five minutes eating. To make these cute confetti cake toppers, all you need is parchment paper, confetti shreds, a hot glue gun, and of course, five minutes. See the full tutorial at AUNT PEACHES: HTTP://WWW.AUNTPEACHES.COM/2013/02/ CONFETTI-CAKE-TOPPERS_13.HTML

❻ These illuminating candle votives are perfect for a summer lawn party and will have the fireflies feeling right at home. Gather up some fabric strips, glue, and a jar, and learn how to make your own at FELLOW FELLOW: HTTP://FELLOWFELLOW. COM/SWEET-DIY-VOTIVES/

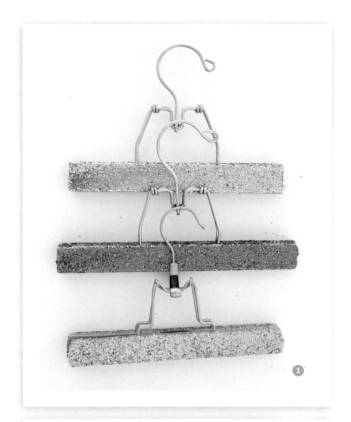

fabric

BECOMING FAMILIAR WITH FABRIC as a crafting material is like getting used to your feet before learning how to walk. Fabric is used, in some form or another, in the vast majority of craft projects, home projects, and design pieces—it can cover, shape, and transform a room. Fabric styles, textures, and patterns set the tone for most of our lives, from the fabrics that cover our bodies to the ones on which we rest our feet.

GETTING TO KNOW *your fabric*

Can I tell you my favorite thing about fabric? It is very forgiving—totally and gratefully forgiving! Crafting with fabric will open new worlds for you by allowing you to try techniques and designs you never dreamed possible, all while giving you the freedom to recover from stumbles along the way.

The weave of the fabric you choose will determine much about how your final project will turn out. Getting to know the different types of weaves, and how to work with each, will allow you to create successful fabric projects time and time again. The end results will also be better aligned with that Pinterest photo that made you want to buy the yard of fabric in the first place! Here are six commonly used fabric weaves:

❶ BASIC OR PLAIN WEAVE: The vast majority of fabrics are made out of a plain weave. It is smooth in texture and holds patterns well. It cuts easily and is a good choice for most beginner projects. Two common plain weaves are tweed and broadcloth.

❷ RIBBED WEAVE: You'll see ribbed weaves most often in knit and crochet fabrics. It is recognizable by the parallel lines left in the fabric.

❸ BASKETWEAVE: The most popular basketweave fabric is burlap. It has a looser, more rustic weave, and is a great option for larger projects like tablecloths and curtains. The fabric is very easy to cut, but because of the weave, can be difficult to sew and glue. This type of weave will often leave a mess of fabric dust behind after being worked with, which is easily avoided by gently misting it with water before crafting.

❹ TWILL WEAVE: Twill weave is a mainstay of denim, herringbone, and other sturdy fabrics, and it is distinguishable by diagonal lines on a fabric. It is great for projects that see a lot of wear and tear such as pillows, purses, and chair covers.

❺ SATIN WEAVE: Satin weave is known for its gorgeous drape. It is a good choice for projects where sheen and flow are important. It is the most difficult fabric to cut evenly, as it frays easily and can slide around on the cutter. A good tip for cutting this type of fabric is to place it on a sheet of tissue paper and cut through both layers together. This will give substance to the weave and give your rotary cutter something to grip to, to keep it from slipping around as you run through it.

❻ PILE WEAVE: Pile weave fabrics have an extra layer of thread placed on the loop— velvet and corduroy fabrics are prime examples. Cutting this type of fabric with too much pressure can make it look flat or bald. To revive the pile, you can gently brush it back into shape.

THREE TIPS FOR DIY TABLE LINENS

We have a very long table in our house that I just adore: It is the perfect spot for hosting a dinner party, all of the kids' friends can fit around it for a birthday, plus it makes our little family of four feel like kings and queens when we're sitting around it for a weeknight meal. Unfortunately, the table isn't a normal size for linens, and special-size tablecloths and runners (or pretty ones in general) can cost a small fortune. As a result, I've taken to making my own, and it's such a breeze. Here are three tips I've found that will help you make great home-sewn linens:

1 USE A CANVAS DROP CLOTH. I love the look of natural table settings, and I've recently found the cheapest way to produce this look is with a canvas drop cloth. One to fit my table cost a whopping $13 at my local hardware store. It can be used on its own for a lived-in linen feel, or it can easily be painted with foam brushes and fabric paint for a more festive vibe as seen in the photo opposite.

2 BUY FABRIC BY THE YARD TO MAKE A PERFECT TABLE RUNNER. From pretty florals and graphic patterns to rich textures like velvet, a yard or two of fabric is usually pretty affordable, and it's the perfect width to fold into thirds for a custom table runner. To make one, measure your table and add 10" (25 cm) on each end. Purchase one length of fabric to match that length. Fold the fabric in thirds along the long sides and iron the folds. Use a small running stitch (see page 81), or even iron-on hemming to finish the fabric and create your own custom runner.

3 LAYER AND TRIM YOUR LINENS. A trick I've been using lately is to layer different fabrics and trim together to top my table. I adore the look and the texture it brings to a room. Even if you have linens that fit your table, create a vibrant design by layering them together—it gives an eclectic and unique effect. Just overlap each layer or element about one third of the way through the table and add ribbons, pom-poms, and other trim as you go. And it's a great way to make use of a collection of vintage cloth and thrifted runners!

Filled with all kinds of goodies, these typographic paper bags turn any statement into a festive centerpiece for your next gathering. Make your own by tracing letters onto colored paper bags, cutting out the shapes, and hot gluing extra paper strips to the sides to round out the letters. See the full tutorial at A Subtle Revelry: http://asubtlerevelry.com/

hanging fabric magazine rack

SKILL LEVEL: Beginner
TIME NEEDED: 60 minutes

Corralling all your favorite magazines is simple with this pretty hanging rack. It is a nice touch for an office or den and gets the paper piles off the ground in style. Choosing a bright or textured fabric to work with will make the rack look more like a work of art than a utilitarian storage unit.

SUPPLIES

23 x 30" (58 x 76 cm) piece of fabric per rack (I used a polka-dot
    burlap, but any basic, twill, or basketweave will work)
Measuring tape
Iron
Ironing board
Sewing machine or hand-sewing needle
Thread to match fabric
Fabric scissors
Two ¼" (6 mm) diameter wooden dowels,
    cut to 36" (91 cm) long or curtain rods
One set of double curtain rod brackets
Pencil
Screwdriver

INSTRUCTIONS

1 Working from the short end, fold the fabric over 2" (5 cm) to create a rod pocket opening. Iron the fold and sew into place with a straight stitch (see page 81) about ⅜" (1 cm) in from the edge of the fabric, leaving the pocket open on both short sides. Repeat on the opposite short end of the fabric to create a second pocket. Run a wooden dowel or curtain rod through each opening.

2 Decide where you'd like to hang your rack, and measure out the curtain bracket placement. Be sure to allow for about 1" (2.5 cm) of overhang on each side to stabilize the rack. Mark the placement lightly in pencil.

3 Install the curtain brackets in the positions you marked, following the manufacturer's instructions. Hang the magazine rack in the bracket, placing one dowel in each well of the bracket. Tighten each rod into place with the curtain rod screws, if necessary.

fabric-lined shelves

SKILL LEVEL: Advanced
TIME NEEDED: 180 minutes

Having space to showcase and store your possessions not only helps with the clutter, but also brings a festive design note to any room. Purchasing pre-made shelves is fine and all, but I find that they all look a bit similar and bland after a while. Creating your own shelves with wood and fabric makes a much nicer statement in a home. Plus, it can bring color and texture to a part of the wall that needs a reason to pop.

SUPPLIES

Measuring tape

Fabric scissors

Thick cotton or textured fabric

A piece of pine cut to the dimensions
of your space (for this project, I used
both 1 x 12 x 24" [2 x 30 x 61 cm] and
1 x 12 x 36" [2 x 30 x 91 cm] pieces)

Pencil

Embroidery thread (optional)

Embroidery needle (optional)

Fabric glue

Stud finder (optional)

Two wall brackets

Power screwdriver

1½ or 2" (4- or 5-cm) drywall screws

#8 x ¾" (2-cm) wood screws

INSTRUCTIONS

❶ Start by measuring and cutting the fabric. To cover
the entire shelf, measure the length of the shelf and
multiply it by 2.5. To cover just the top, simply add an
extra 2" (5 cm).

❷ If you choose to embroider your shelves, measure out
where you'd like your text to appear, pencil in your
words or design, and embroider following the steps
on page 81.

❸ Apply a small layer of fabric glue on the top of the
shelf and along the back side. Lay the fabric along
the shelf and gently smooth out any wrinkles with
your fingers. Turn the shelf over and fold the fabric
back as you would when wrapping a present. Use the
glue to firm down and fold into place, taking special
care that the corners are brought in correctly.

❹ Let the glue dry and set for 24 hours.

❺ Locate the studs in the wall to hang your brackets.
(You could use a fancy stud finder from the hardware store, or use the "pound the wall and listen
for different sounds" method. I recommend the
stud finder.) Using a power screwdriver, attach
the brackets to the wall at the studs using your
drywall screws.

❻ Place the shelf on the brackets, and screw into
the wood from below using your wood screws.

removable fabric wallpaper

SKILL LEVEL: Intermediate
TIME NEEDED: 90 minutes

Wallpaper is making a huge comeback in home décor today, and rightly so—there's nothing better than being surrounded by walls covered with texture, color, and design. Wallpaper can set the mood in a room like nothing else. There are a few downsides to wallpaper, though. Besides the obvious expense, it is also hard to install and most styles are nearly impossible to remove.

Instead of committing to wallpaper, why not use fabric? The process of putting fabric up on the walls is simple and affordable, and you can remove it in a jiffy if the landlords are coming over and you "forgot" to tell them you were making some improvements! I love the look, especially inside a closet or along the hallway.

SUPPLIES

Fabric scissors
Fabric to cover the wall space (any kind of light weight will work, although the thicker the fabric, the longer the soaking and drying times will be)
Large bowl
Liquid fabric stiffener (see note)
Sponge, for smoothing as you go

NOTE: *Small bottles of liquid fabric stiffener can be purchased at your local craft store. However, if you are doing a large wall, I would suggest ordering a gallon-size bottle online.*

INSTRUCTIONS

❶ Begin by cutting the fabric into manageable strips for hanging. I find the best lengths to work with are 24 x 48" (61 x 122 cm). If you are covering a large area, be sure to cut the fabric at a good place to break and match the pattern on each strip.

❷ Fill a large bowl with the fabric stiffener. Dredge the fabric strips one at a time in the fabric stiffener, making sure each piece is thoroughly coated. Squeeze to remove excess liquid before hanging.

❸ Hang the fabric on the wall just like you would hang wallpaper. (You can follow the instructions on page 75 for hanging the contact paper wallpaper.) Start at the top corner of the wall and be sure the fabric strip is hanging straight (I always use a second set of hands for this part). Gently begin smoothing down the section of the wall with your hands, straightening as you go.

❹ Once the basic hang is complete, dip the sponge into the fabric stiffener and run it along the fabric to smooth out any kinks and to ensure all the edges are wet and lying flat. Do this on each section once after hanging, and then again over the entire wall once it has been completely covered.

❺ Allow to dry completely before hanging or resting any items against the wall.

❻ When it comes time to remove the wallpaper, do so by gently lifting one side with a finger and pulling down. Wash the wall with a gentle cleanser to remove any leftover stiffener, and the room will be back to new instantly!

love
is when
a girl puts on perfume
and a boy puts on
shaving cologne and
they go out and
smell
each other

more projects to try

❶ This fort structure is perfect to set up camp in your backyard, but can easily be used for evening adventures inside, too! Make your own with sheer tab curtains, twine, and large wooden dowels, which are easy to find at your local craft store. See the full tutorial at A SUBTLE REVELRY: HTTP://ASUBTLEREVELRY.COM/FORT-BUILDING-101

❷ These scripted pillowcases are a pretty way to celebrate love, home, and those special moments of rest we all treasure. Make your own by scribbling a cherished poem or saying onto white cotton or jersey pillowcases with a fabric marker. See the full tutorial at A SUBTLE REVELRY: HTTP://ASUBTLEREVELRY.COM/SCRIPTED-PILLOWS

❸ Creating the elegant look of long-stemmed fabric flowers is easy with the use of fabric, thread, and glue. Make your own by cutting scallops into strips of fabric, sewing off the edges, and circling the strips around a wooden stem into a rose shape. See the full tutorial at SNOWY BLISS: HTTP://SNOWYBLISS.BLOGSPOT.COM/2010/06/LONG-STEMMED-FABRIC-FLOWERS.HTML

❹ With just a few stitches on your sewing machine, you can make these adorable fabric bags for all your small gifts. All you need is fabric paint, a stamp kit, and some leftover fabric you have buried away in your craft closet. See the full tutorial at LOTTS & LOTS: /HTTP://LOTTSAND LOTS.BLOGSPOT.CO.UK/2013/04/DIY-PAINTED-FABRIC-GIFT-BAGS.HTML

❺ Recycle old scarves, shirts, and other clothing items you love by creating your own, pretty fabric tape! Extend the life of your favorite fabrics with just a bit of acrylic sealant and masking tape. See the full tutorial at A SUBTLE REVELRY: HTTP://ASUBTLEREVELRY.COM/FABRIC-TAPE-DIY

❶

159

metal

METAL MAKES A BIG IMPACT. But even with its long history of bringing beauty into the home, its massive, heavy qualities can make it seem like a daunting material for beginner crafters. Don't let it scare you away—exposed lines, rough materials, and industrial features are all the rage lately, making metal the perfect decorative element for updating your home.

METALS YOU NEED to know

Many different types of metals can be used for craft projects, but there are five that I always find myself coming back to:

ALUMINUM

Aluminum is the most abundant metal on the planet, hence why we use it to package soda and other pantry staples. It's a great metal for crafting because it's soft, heat-resistant, and flexible, making it easy to mold and shape. I even use it in wire form for an assortment of different projects.

NICKEL

This hard metal is corrosion-resistant, which means it won't rust or degrade when exposed to the elements. Because of this, it is often used in jewelry-making, but I also love to include it in my patio and garden projects, since I know it will withstand the outdoor elements.

SILVER

This is one of my favorite metals to use in projects for parties and events. Although it is a more expensive material than its counterparts, the bright shine of polished silver is a look that will never go out of style. I especially love the look of solid silver decorations on the table at a dinner party, or silver punched with a monogram to top a gift with classy style.

COPPER

Copper is the prettiest of all the metals, in my opinion, and popular design seems to agree—there is nothing as gorgeous as exposed copper plumbing for a bathtub. The metal is soft and easy to use, making it another perfect candidate for beginners. In plate form it can be cut, punched, and molded to create wreaths, ornaments, and even cake stands! In pipe form, you can stack it to create very pretty bowls.

STEEL

Until recently, steel did not get much attention in the crafting world. Because it is tougher and more difficult to work with, it was not seen as an amateur material. But with the popularity of pipe fittings, and the ease of pre-cut lengths and connectors that you can grab at your local hardware store, this metal is quickly securing its place on the home DIY scene. I love the industrial look of pipe-fitted candlesticks and other easy-to-assemble home accessories.

SAFETY TIPS

Before we get started on the projects, here are a few safety tips for working with metal:

❶ Always wear working gloves. Never run your finger along the side of any pipe or metal piece—it is likely to be very sharp and can cause injury.

❷ After cutting pipes or strapping, have a piece of thick paper handy to "sweep" the area you are working with to prevent any small slivers from attacking your skin.

❸ Always make sure your pipes are securely screwed together and in alignment to ensure the safety of the finished piece. Use a wrench when necessary—no toppling racks around here!

GETTING TO KNOW YOUR JOINTS AND BARS

Metal piping is actually very simple to work with. By hand-screwing pieces together, you can make high-level design projects fairly easily. Part of the fear comes from not knowing the lingo, but below I've outlined eight basic pipe fittings that will help guide you through purchasing the materials for most pipe projects.

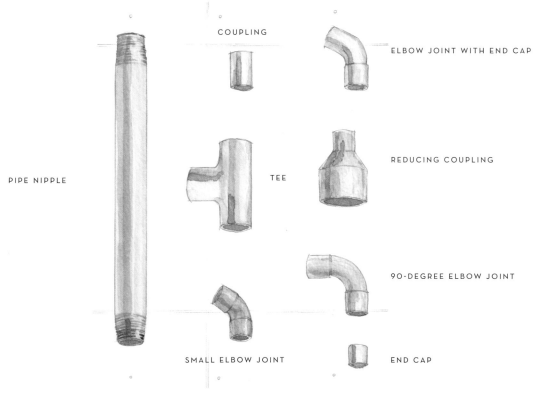

COUPLING

ELBOW JOINT WITH END CAP

REDUCING COUPLING

PIPE NIPPLE

TEE

90-DEGREE ELBOW JOINT

SMALL ELBOW JOINT

END CAP

hanging metal garden globes

SKILL LEVEL: Intermediate
TIME NEEDED: 15 minutes per globe

Bringing your garden inside, or designing it well outside, is easy with these simple metal globes. They look pretty on their own, but even better with a small potted plant in the middle. They also make great trailing guides for ivy and other garden plants. A collection on a large windowsill would look amazing!

SUPPLIES

At least two packs of 1" (2.5 cm) wide
 perforated metal hanger straps
Cylindrical object, for shaping (see note)
Wire cutters
One #8 (32 x ⅜" [81 x 1 cm]) screw and nut
 for each terra-cotta pot (optional)
Terra-cotta flowerpot (optional)
String or fishing wire, for hanging

NOTE: *I used a jar to mold the smaller globe and a beach ball to mold the larger one.*

INSTRUCTIONS

1. Measure out your strapping by wrapping it around your shaping object and cutting it to size using wire cutters. Repeat with three more lengths of strapping.

2. Overlap the first circle of strapping with the second circle, making an "X" shape. Place a screw through one of the top holes to temporarily hold the two pieces together.

3. Place the third circle of strapping over the first two to create a sphere. Bolt the top screw and a bottom screw into place.

4. If you plan to place a terra-cotta pot inside, do this before wrapping the last strap. Once the third circle is attached, remove the bottom screw and replace it with a slightly longer screw. Set the terra-cotta pot atop the screw before replacing the nut with a larger one to hold the pot in place.

5. Wrap the fourth length so it lays horizontally across the midsection and add a screw at every point the horizontal strapping intersects with the vertical pieces.

6. Fill your pot with small flowers and herbs and hang with a length of string or fishing wire for a modern garden display.

metal candlesticks

SKILL LEVEL: Beginner
TIME NEEDED: 30 minutes

Metal candlesticks remind me that simplicity is often the most beautiful route to take when choosing items for your home. With their modern nod to the industrial past, they are an item I could see using for years throughout every style shift I may encounter.

SUPPLIES

One 4 to 10" (10 to 25 cm) -long and ½" (12-mm) -diameter pipe nipple (you can mix and match when making more than one candleholder)
One ½" (12-mm) floor flange
One ½" (12-mm) coupling
One 10 to 15" (25- to 38-cm) taper candle

NOTE: *For this project, both ¼" (6-mm) and ½" (12-mm) pipe nipples and couplings are suitable. Or get crazy and make a few of each!*

INSTRUCTIONS

1 Connect the pipe nipple and the floor flange together and top with the coupling—there is no adhesive required for this project!

2 Gently "screw" in your candle of choice and place around the house for a stunning display.

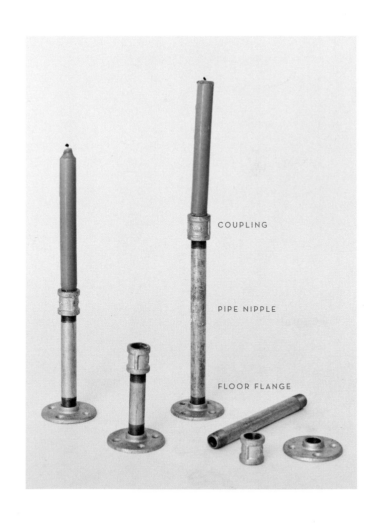

COUPLING

PIPE NIPPLE

FLOOR FLANGE

metal clothes rack

SKILL LEVEL: Advanced
TIME NEEDED: 120 minutes

Who doesn't wish they had one extra hanging bar in their closet to keep their favorite pieces in sight? Fortunately, metal clothes racks are easier to make than they look. They are comprised of a combination of metal pieces that are screwed together. With only a simple switch of the long pipe dimensions, they are endlessly customizable, making it easy to create a new pipe clothing rack that is perfect for your space. I wrapped this one with yarn on one side for a more feminine look, but you can leave it plain if your décor is more sparse.

SUPPLIES

Two ¾" (2-cm) 90-degree elbows
Two ¾ x 30" (2 x 76 cm) steel pipes
Two ¾ x 48" (2 x 122 cm) steel pipes
Four ¾" (2-cm) tees
Four ¾ x 8" (2 x 20 cm) steel pipe nipples
Two ¾ x 2½" (2 x 6 cm) steel pipe nipples
Four ¾" (2-cm) 90-degree street elbows
Four ¾" (2-cm) galvanized floor flanges
Yarn, in assorted colors (optional)

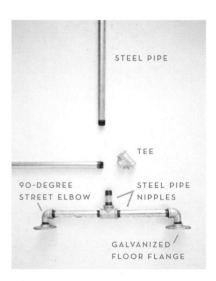

STEEL PIPE

TEE

90-DEGREE
STREET ELBOW

STEEL PIPE
NIPPLES

GALVANIZED
FLOOR FLANGE

INSTRUCTIONS

❶ Screw one 90-degree elbow into each side of one of the 30" (76-cm) steel pipes, making sure each elbow lines up facing the same direction.

❷ Screw a 48" (122-cm) steel pipe into each side (it should look like a "U" at this point).

❸ Screw a tee onto each 48" (122-cm) steel pipe. Each tee opening should be facing the other tee opening.

❹ Screw the remaining 30" (76-cm) steel pipe into the tee on the left as completely as possible. Align the right side with the open tee, and tighten it 4 or 5 times. This will allow it to be snug on both sides of the bar.

❺ To create the bases, screw two 8" (20-cm) steel pipe nipples onto the two straight sides of a tee. Screw a 2½" (6-cm) steel pipe nipple onto the top of the tee. Screw a 90-degree street elbow onto each open side of the 8" (20-cm) nipples, making sure they are facing the same direction on each side. Screw two galvanized floor flanges to each street elbow. Repeat the process to create a base for the opposite side.

❻ Screw each base onto the open ends of the two tees on each side of the structure.

❼ Take a picture and put it on social media: You just made a metal clothes rack all by your bad self!

FABULOUS PARTY STYLE

Having a wardrobe that is always party ready can
seem intimidating, even with a beautiful clothing
rack (see page 168) on which to display it. But just
as I enjoy crafting a beautiful home, I like to give
my clothes the same treatment. Here are a few items
I keep on hand for a quick and pretty party look.

A LENGTH OF SEQUINS: Easily stored, a strip
of sequins can be used as a belt to fancy up a dress,
tied around the wrist as a bracelet, or run along
a headband for an instant lift to your hair.

A SMALL JAR OF GLITTER: A must on my vanity.
It can add a bit of sparkle to my hair, on my eyes, or
even update a drab-looking pair of shoes for a fun
night out on the town.

A FLORAL SCARF: This does double-duty as a pretty
hair tie, or creates a statement piece as a sash bow on
a ho-hum clutch. Plus, I adore how a pretty scarf can
update any dress and make it spring-party ready.

SATIN RIBBONS: There aren't many crafting
problems a wide length of satin ribbon won't solve.
Tie a ribbon around your heels for a big bow effect,
fashion one into a necklace or bracelet, or even
stitch one around the hem of a dress to add a bit
of length as needed.

more projects to try

HERE ARE MORE INSPIRING METAL PROJECTS FROM MY OWN BLOG, *A SUBTLE REVELRY*, AS WELL AS SOME OF MY FAVORITE BLOGS:

❶ Why go out searching for an overpriced copper light fixture when you can build one yourself? Deck out your dining, living, and bedrooms with this awesome pendant made of copper piping. See the full tutorial at DESIGN MILK: HTTP://DESIGN-MILK.COM/MAKE-IT-MODERN-DIY-COPPER-GEOMETRIC-PENDANT-LAMP/

❷ Introduce a touch of metal into your home with this copper vase. Made from copper pipe covered with air-dry clay, it's the perfect vessel for your prettiest flower findings. See the full tutorial at THE FELTED FOX: HTTP://THEFELTEDFOX.BLOGSPOT.COM/2013/04/COPPER-VASE-DIY.HTML

❸ A metal towel holder is such a fun way to compliment a kitchen counter. With Molly's printable wood base template and some copper piping, you can screw your own into place in no time. See the full tutorial at ALMOST MAKES PERFECT: HTTP://WWW.ALMOSTMAKESPERFECT.COM/2014/03/18/DIY-COPPER-WOOD-PAPER-TOWEL-HOLDER/

❹ With metal-coated paper (the easiest type of metal to work with) and wood veneer, you can add a beautiful metallic element to your nightly wind down. See the full tutorial for these accented candles by Michelle Edgemont at A SUBTLE REVELRY: HTTP://ASUBTLEREVELRY.COM/WOODEN-AND-GOLD-CANDLES

❺ Put your green thumb to work as you make these adorable garden plant markers out of old soda cans and a metal stamping set! Get creative with your herbs, fruits and veggies, and see the full tutorial at GREY LUSTER GIRL: HTTP://GREYLUSTERGIRL.COM/DIY-GARDEN-PLANT-MARKERS/

❻ Start your next party off right with some tasty appetizers! Assemble your own mini tabletop grills by using an old terra-cotta planter, a couple of small adjustable metal cake tins, and wire mesh. These are perfect for grilling little sliders, kabobs, or even marshmallows. See the full tutorial at A SUBTLE REVELRY: HTTP://ASUBTLEREVELRY.COM/TABLE-TOP-GRILL

RESOURCES

The materials and tools used in the projects in this book are generally available at craft, art supply, and hardware stores nationwide. If you cannot find what you are looking for locally, try these online resources.

FOR AFFORDABLE WAX SUPPLIES:
Amazon.com

FOR A VAST SELECTION OF CONCRETE:
HomeDepot.com

FOR GRAPHIC FABRIC:
Spoonflower.com

FOR AN UNMATCHED PAINT SELECTION AND CARDBOARD LETTER MOLDS:
Joann.com

FOR METAL CUTTING SUPPLIES:
Whimsic.com

FOR GENERAL CRAFT TOOLS AND MATERIALS:
DickBlick.com

ACKNOWLEDGMENTS

First and foremost, I need to thank my husband, Matt, who played a huge part in creating this book. From pouring concrete to editing to reminding me to stop and eat, his partnership was essential to completing this project, as it is with everything I do.

To my mom, who taught me from an early age that I could do anything I wanted. I craft, I write, I blog because of your lessons.

I'd also like to thank Jocelyn Noel, who photographed all the projects. Her talent—and eye—are a treasure to me.

I'm grateful to Amanda Waggoner for her illustrations. I am so pleased to share her work with you in this form.

This book would not have been possible without the crafting assistance of Tenny Vaughn, Ashley Ingle, and Christina Lang, who spent many mornings with me completing projects and styling for shoots. Thanks, girls!

I'd like to thank my readers, who've tried and tested my projects. You inspired this book, and the text inside is a response to every comment and email I've received from you.

I'm also grateful to my editors, Rebecca Kaplan and Cristina Garces, who patiently walked me through the new process of writing for a book (and not a blog), and to everyone at Abrams for giving this concept a chance.

A special thanks to book designer Sarah Gifford, who made my material come to life.

And finally, thanks to my kids, for putting up with a mom who was often buried in glue guns, edits, and glitter.